COLT
GUNS

COLT GUNS

By MARTIN RYWELL

COACHWHIP PUBLICATIONS
Greenville, Ohio

Colt Guns, by Martin Rywell
© 2023 Coachwhip Publications edition

First published 1953 / 1957 reprint
Dr. Martin M. Rywell, 1905-1972
CoachwhipBooks.com

Cover image: Colt Model 1851 Navy Percussion Revolver
Metropolitan Museum of Modern Art, Gift of John E. Parsons, 1968

ISBN 1-61646-564-6
ISBN-13 978-1-61646-564-3

CONTENTS

Chapter   *Page*

1. Samuel Colt, biographical sketch by Martin Rywell 5
2. Rotating Chambered-Breech Firearms by Samuel Colt 18
3. Testimony Before Parliament Committee (Extracts) by Samuel Colt 50
4. The Colt Revolver in 1863 by J. D. Butler 57
5. Visit to Colt Armory in 1863 by Henry Barnard 61
6. U. S. Army and Navy Orders of Colt Arms, 1841 to 1857 66
7. Colt Arms Manufactured from 1856 to 1865 68
8. Manual for Colt Revolvers 69
9. Letter to Samuel Colt's Son by I. W. Stuart 73
10. On the Death of Samuel Colt by L. H. Sigourney 75
11. Did Colt Invent the Revolver? by Martin Rywell 78
12. Antique Colt Arms and Their Current Prices 84
13. History of Firearms by Martin Rywell 94
14. Etymology of Firearms Terms by Martin Rywell 97
15. Illustrations 98

To determine current 1957 market values of antique
Colt guns, add 50% to prices listed on pages 84
through 93.

CHAPTER ONE

SAMUEL COLT

By MARTIN RYWELL

JUSTICE AND COLT
(*Harper's Weekly*—June 29, 1878)

"Thrice is he armed that hath his quarrel just."
  Ah, Shakespeare, that might do
For those good knights who now are dust,
  Those swords now rusted through

But we who live a keener life
  They triple armor bolt:
And for defense, as well as strife,
  Are six time armed by Colt.

The great awakening of science in the seventeenth and eighteenth century was the turning point of history. It began when free institutions were in the ascendency and a vast continent rich in natural resources was opened to all.

The impact of inventions that ushered in the technical industrial civilization accelerated the continuity of accumulations that belonged to the world. It received its greatest impetus and contribution from American mass-production. The saga of the technical ingenuity of weapon production methods supplied the details.

The pattern was set by Eli Whitney's design of interchangeable parts for musket manufacture. It was his government contract in 1798 for 10,000 muskets of model 1795 that created the challenging problem. Colt applied and extended the experience of Eli Whitney and set the pattern for modern world industry.

Every American has heard of the Colt revolver. Few know the story of the incredible life of Samuel Colt who was a good deal more than just the inventor of the first successful repeating firearm.

Much of his life was a struggle for money to enable him to prove his invention a success, and to buck the inertia of our military system. He constantly manipulated to keep going. It began with his amusing career as Dr. Coult, laughing gas chemist, to finance production of the working models of his invention. It continued as he quarreled with his backers about his expenses; was arrested for debt and saw his first company—The Patent Arms Manufacturing Company of Paterson, New Jersey fail. Nothing could deter his passionate conviction in his invention. No one could take his patent away from him.

Samuel Colt was born in Hartford, Connecticut, July 19, 1814, the fifth of six children to Christopher and Sarah Caldwell Colt. A month before Sam's seventh birthday his mother died of tuberculosis. His father remarried and the children were scattered among relatives. Sam was indentured to a farmer for a year and after the fulfillment of the indenture he went to work in his father's newly established dyeing and bleaching factory in Ware, Massachusetts.

Sam liked to try original chemical mixtures and their reactions. It was fascinating and William T. Smith, the company's chemist encouraged him. It was man's duty to investigate every phenomenon of nature and utilize every resource. That epitomized the late Eighteenth Century and proclaimed it the age of reason. Knowledge of the natural world was to set men free and man has arrived at an enlightened point in history when men could be free. Man's outlook had changed.

Samuel Colt attended Amherst Academy, a college preparatory school in Amherst, Massachusetts which had obtained a reputation for the teaching of chemistry which was then just beginning to be studied. Amherst Academy and Amherst College were not connected, though the students of the Academy could attend college lectures on chemistry. The scientific teachers then at Amherst College were second to none. Among them were Edward Hitchcock, Charles Upham Shepard, Amos Eaton, Ebenezer S. Snell and Charles B. Adams. Samuel Colt was exposed to the influence of these giants who blazed the path for science in the United States.

Sam was not quite 15 when he made his first invention—a discovery that he could explode gunpowder with electricity. His dramatic announcement was a handbill that informed in bold type that "Samuel Colt will blow a raft sky high on Ware Pond, July 4, 1829."

A waterproofed gunpowder charge detonated by a tarred wire that led to a Leyden jar on shore was his simple machine. The inspiration had come from Grandpa Caldwell's story of "Bushnell's Marine Turtle" used in the Revolutionary War and the song his mother sang, "The Battle of the Keys."

David Bushnell was a Connecticut Yankee who graduated from Yale in 1775. He had the idea that a machine would blow up vessels from under water. Shortly after graduation he constructed one to be used against the British. Several pieces of oak timber were scooped out and fitted together in the shape of a round clam. It was bound with iron bands. The seams were caulked. Then it was tarred to make it airtight. It was large enough to contain one engineer. The top had glass to enable the engineer to read. Several hundred pounds of lead kept it upright and gave it buoyance. It could move vertically by means of pumps and horizontally by paddles. It contained over one hundred pounds of gunpowder which could be discharged at enemy vessels. It became known as "Bushnell's Turtle." Bushnell tried his invention out on several British ships in New York harbor and in Delaware, between August 1776 and December 1777 without success. In desperation Bushnell prepared a number of machines in kegs to be floated by the tide to British vessels.

These exploded without much damage but with great alarm to the British. Bushnell's efforts earned ridicule and laughter from his countrymen. Samuel Colt received the sparks from Bushnell's invention and his imagination was aflame with electrically controlled mine. Samuel Colt would succeed where David Bushnell failed.

Many came that July 4th to be entertained by exhibition; they were curious and it was a holiday but one young man was motivated by interest. He was Elisha K. Root, a mechanic from Chicopee Falls and the inventor of several machines. His life line was to become entwined with that of Samuel Colt but future was shielded from both on that July 4th. Twenty years later Root became superintendent of Colt's plant and invented many improvements in Colt arms. After Colt's death, Root assumed the presidency of Colt's Armory. That July 4th they knew nothing about the future and were interested in Samuel Colt's invention. The mine exploded but the raft had drifted and only mud flew "sky high" and onto holiday raiment.

The idea didn't explode. Samuel Colt had a constitutional stubbornness which was the passion to communicate the discovery of his imagination and to translate it into reality.

The invention a failure, his father sent Sam to sea and on August 2, 1830, Sam apprenticed as a plain seaman to Captain Spaulding sailed from Boston bound for London and Calcutta on the brig, "Corlo."

In the meantime the development of the percussion system of ignition was taking place. A Scotch clergyman, Reverend Alexander Forsyth, had dabbled in chemistry as a hobby. A number of chemical substances, such as fulminates of mercury and silver, and mixtures containing potassium chloride had the qualities of instantaneous explosion when struck. Forsyth invented a percussion lock in 1807 which was a practical application of this chemical principle. It was a gun lock in which a minute quantity of fulminate of mercury was exploded by the blow of a small firing pin which was struck by the hammer. The fire of the priming was transmitted to the main charge through a vent. The practical application of this system was successfully developed by Joshua Shaw of Philadelphia. In 1816 he received a patent for the invention of a copper percussion cap containing fulminate of mercury which was placed on a hollow cone or nipple, and when struck by the hammer, flashed the fire into the main charge and exploded it in the breech. Percussion ignition had arrived though it did not come into general use until the second quarter of the nineteenth century.

The multi-barreled pistol or revolver was known as early as the 1500's and many ingenious forms of a revolving breech that could be fired in succession were on display in many museums. In 1818 Elisha Collier of Boston, Massachusetts, invented a clever revolving cylinder flintlock. In 1824 he went to England to manufacture and market it because he could not find a market at home. The drawback was the cumbersome flintlock ignition; it took a long time between the pressing of the trigger and the ball discharge; it interfered with steady aim; it became impossible to ignite in wet or inclement weather. The inability to ignite in wet weather gave birth to the phrase, "Keep your powder dry." These objections to flintlock were remedied by the practical invention of percussion ignition in 1807.

The problem of designing a gun that would shoot more than once without reloading was an ancient one. An answer that was tried as early as the 16th century was the binding together of several hand guns. Other answers developed with several barrels, several loads in a single barrel, and a cylinder with several holes as barrels. They revolved manually.

Attempted solution of the problem of multishot weapons began with matchlock ignition and continued through wheel-lock and flintlock. These ignition systems in common depended upon a spark ignition of the priming powder outside of the chamber. This made possible the ignition and explosion of more than one chamber simultaneously.

Percussion ignition was the solution. The basic principles of multishot had been developed. Percussion sanctioned their safety. Aboard ship Samuel Colt's imagination throbbed with the idea of a multi-shot percussion firearm, and the idea commanded reality as Sam whittled a model out of a wooden tackle. The whittled wooden model cocked the hammer and thus automatically revolved the cylinder in line with the barrel and there locked it while the shot was fired. Beneath the accidental fulfillment there was continuity that evolved through the centuries. It was a pure flash of momentary imagination and our power is in our imaginations.

Upon Sam's return home from Calcutta, he had working models made by a gunsmith but they failed. Sam needed money to continue with his experiments to successfully complete his invention and he decided to earn it by demonstrating laughing gas.

Humphrey Davy in 1800 discovered nitrous oxide or "laughing gas." The effects of this gas produced an intoxicating sensation with "an agreeable sense of well-being."

Samuel Colt, aged 18, left Ware, Massachusetts, to subdue a cruel world with laughing gas. Not as Samuel Colt but as Dr. Coult, chemist, late of New York, London and Calcutta. Titles give testimony and rank is ritual for authority. Samuel Colt understood that bit of showmanship psychology. So self-conferred, he assumed the title of doctor. Later in life from the same source came the rank of Colonel.

Prestige of geography is likewise important. The impressive stamp of address was necessary raiment. The addresses—New York, London and Calcutta—lent enchantment and signified international approval. Later in life Samuel Colt used New York and London addresses for similar effect. Fine plumage makes fine birds.

People were interested in self-improvement. They were anxious to know about the newly discovered facts of nature and science. They wanted to see practical applications of science.

Dr. Coult went from town to town. When he came to a town he set up the portable laboratory with its variety of chemical jars and mysterious apparatus to create the illusion of science on a busy street corner. Then he invited a volunteer to inhale "laughing gas" as the passers-by watched what happened. The demonstration over, Sam took up a collection.

From the collection culled from the crowd on the New England common, Samuel Colt climbed to Boston's Masonic Hall on June 22, 1832. It meant added prestige. Editorial notices indicate that he travelled to widely separated and large communities. In 1833 he lectured at Wheeling, West Virginia, Pittsburgh, Pennsylvania, Rochester and Albany in New York. In 1834 he stopped at Winchester, Virginia, Charleston, South Carolina, Augusta, Georgia, Albany, New York and then on to Canada. In Canada he stopped at Montreal, Quebec, St. Johns and returned to Lowell, Massachusetts. In 1835 he visited Petersburg, Virginia in February.

From behind a plush curtain came Dr. Coult, distinguished chemist of New York, London and Calcutta, his appearance dignified by mustache, beard, frock coat and high hat. A contempary news account relates that after inhaling his "airs from heaven," Samuel Colt sang "The Merry Swiss Boy." That was Samuel Colt from ages eighteen to twenty-one. The proceeds of these lectures enabled him to hire a mechanic in Baltimore to make up experimental revolvers while he toured the country. He kept sending the mechanic money or promises to continue the work.

In July 1835 Samuel Colt, now twenty-one and of legal age, gave up his lecture tours, borrowed $1,000 from an aunt, went to London and Paris, and obtained foreign patents on the revolver. Upon his return to the United States in 1836 he obtained a United States patent and proceeded to form a corporation to manufacture Colt guns.

A company was organized. Many prominent capitalists invested cash in the venture that was capitalized at $230,000. Dudley Selden, Samuel Colt's cousin became secretary and general manager. The company began the manufacture of firearms in 1836 in part of a silk mill in Paterson, New Jersey. Samuel Colt's contract with the company was on a royalty basis with the privilege of purchasing stock to the extent of $50,000 within a year. It also provided that the patents would revert to Samuel Colt if and when the company would cease their manufacturing. It started with great expectations.

Friction soon developed. Samuel Colt wanted machinery; wanted the entertainment of persons who would be useful in the sales of firearms; and the presentation of ornate Colt guns to men in important positions. The company objected. They said that his methods were unorthodox. Samuel Colt disregarded their admonitions and lobbied for government acceptance. In 1839 the Army Ordnance Board finally tested his repeating guns and rejected them. The Army pistol then used was calibre 54, smooth bore, single shot flintlock. The Colt revolver was 40 caliber, rifled, 5 shot, percussion and a spare cylinder with another 5 shots which could be quickly substituted.

Samuel Colt then took 100 repeating rifles, carbines and revolvers to Florida where we were then engaged in combat with the Seminole Indians. He wanted to demonstrate the Colt superiority as a weapon in actual combat. Colt sold 50 guns and received a government check of $6,250.00 in payment. He also sold individual officers some revolvers. Colt was indeed happy over this sale and started back home. The boat sailed to St. Augustine, Florida, stuck on a bar and he tried to get ashore in a small boat. The small boat capsized and Samuel Colt lost the check for $6,250.

The happiness over the big sale was short-lived as the government procedure to replace the lost check was an Act of Congress. Cousin Dudley's letter was even sharper. He doubted the veracity of Colt about the check. Eventually the government replaced the check. This was indicative of the sharp misunderstandings between Cousin Dudley for the Company and Samuel Colt.

A depression set in. Sales dwindled. Samuel Colt sued the company and by 1841 the company was bankrupt.

Colt then devoted himself to have the government finance his experiments for a submarine mine for harbor defense. Congress voted him $20,000.

The next venture was due to his meeting Samuel Morse. Colt organized a company and laid the first submarine telegraph cable—a short one in New York City—to announce the approach of ships.

Five years elapsed. General Zachary Taylor was on the border to defend the country against Mexico in the dispute about Texas annexation. Many of the men with General Taylor had used Colt firearms. Captain Sam Walker was one of them and he was sent North to recruit volunteers and to buy 1000 Colt revolvers.

Captain Walker went to Samuel Colt who had no tools, no machines, no patterns, and not even a sample of his own invention—the revolver.

Colt made a wooden working model and persuaded Eli Whitney, Jr., to make them for him at his plant in Whitneyville, Conn. Colt had a contract with Whitney whereby Colt could buy the tools, machines, patterns and parts at the end of the contract.

The Mexican War proved the Colt revolver superiority. He set up a shop in Hartford, Connecticutt and soon had an order for another 1000 revolvers.

Orders flooded him from all over the world. Colt became a world traveller and each trip meant more and more new markets opened for his products.

Colt received international recognition. In 1851 he delivered an address before the Institution of Civil Engineers in London wherein he stressed the manufacture of firearms by machinery. In 1852 Colt established a factory in London. Charles Dickens who visited the plant marveled that so much of the work was done by women who were not skilled mechanics by merely controlled machines by steam power.

In 1854 Colt went to Russia to call on the Czar with presents. The Czar wanted one of his officers to be present in Hartford to inspect the arms being manufactured for him. It was at the time of the Crimean War and passage seemed impossible since England had thrown up a blockade around Russia. Samuel Colt solved the problem. He took the Russian officer to England with him as his valet and brought him safely to Connecticut.

A Committee of Parliament examined Samuel Colt in 1854 on the merits of machine-made weapons and whether they were better and cheaper than the English-fabricated. Colt explained how our industrial development depended upon machinery, interchangeable parts, and mass production. The replacement of the tool in the hand by the tool as part of the mechanism was the genesis of the industrial revolution. The tool as part of the mechanism is the machine which has both driving and transmitting power. Uniformity was the handicap in the transition. Eli Whitney solved that with interchangeable parts. Samuel Colt was applying and extending the industrial processes to the manufacture of arms.

Lord Seymour asked Colt about the reproduction of irregular shapes. Colt explained how Thomas Blanchard had solved the problem by "an undulating motion in the lathe," and added that it produced not only a better gun-stock but "now it costs less for a stock than it does here for the wood." In 1818 Thomas Blanchard, a timid lad from a farm in Sutton, Massachusetts, worked in the Springfield, Massachusetts, Armory, invented a copying lathe for the irregular forms of wooden gun-stocks and thereby introduced a basic principle still in use. Mass production puzzled the committee as well as Colt's system of cost accounting. Samuel Colt had grasped the modern theories of cost accounting. He explained machinery depreciation as a cost factor. He went into the theory of overhead and concluded with the division of the total by the units produced.

They listened since it is lawful to learn even from those one dislikes. The English upper class disliked us. Their visitors called us low-bred boors. They dreaded our democracy, disliked our independence from the colonies, and feared our competition.

Lord Seymour then turned the inquiry and drifted into the reason for the London factory and was it not an attempt to procure government contracts for ordnance. Colt was their match and his reply was, "I have written to Ordnance of what the arms could be made for in England, but not with a view of taking a contract from that department, but to give my impression of what the arms could be made for in this country. I have indorsed that opinion by the statement that I would supply the arms at those prices."

Mr. Geach of the committee went into the question of Colt's patent and asked, "You were induced to open your establishment for the purpose of carrying the work to perfection and getting the largest amount of profit out of it?" That question was the foundation for a series of questions to find our Colt's costs.

"Yes," Colt answered, "and I am now proud of the results of my exertions and can paddle my own canoe."

Of course Samuel Colt sought a profit. His manufacturing project was economic realism and not abstract humanitarianism. Colt was a realist who perceived and exploited his perception that self-interest governs the vast majority. Were the English unaware of this as they were of machine methods.

Geach was out for blood as he asked, "Until 1849 or 1850, even in America you were not successful and made no profit?"

"It was not profitable. I did not make any money till lately. I made none in America until my arms were employed in the service by the energy of the people who first went to Florida, next to Texas, in the wars against the Indians, and finally Mexico, in our war with that country. That completed the reputation of my arm so far as America is concerned."

The Parliament inquiry into Colt's manufacturing methods in interesting for the revelation of a pattern. Accomplishment was achieved in many spheres in America as a mixture of European background influences that blended with native American conditions. This mixture produced a distinctive American product which in turn influenced Europe. It is a see-saw action of tendencies with Europe at one end and the United States at the other end.

The curiosity and interest of many nations were aroused. What is this firearm of which that heroic soldier Captain Walker said, "I would rather face one thousand of the enemy with two hundred and fifty men armed with Colt's Pistols than one thousand men armed with weapons in ordinary use?" Sample orders came from England, France, Russia, Sardinia, Turkey and other nations. The Colt was being recognized. Sam sensed the portent but what good would this belated reward serve since his patent would soon expire and strangers would share in the feast. An extension of his patent rights would be equitable because litigation and economic factors had deterred the full exploitation of his patent. Congress voted an extension of the Colt basic patent for seven years.

1850-midcentury and the fidgety fifties were ushered in. We were growing with a violent velocity. Prosperity stimulated by California gold and new frontiers hid the great unrest. "All is energy and enterprise, everything is in a state of transition, but of rapid improvement, so rapid, indeed, that those who would describe America now would have to correct all in the short space of ten years; for ten years in America is almost equal to a century in the old continent," observed Captain Marryat.

The frontier rolled towards the Pacific. America was on the move. The caravan moved. Covered white-topped wagons rumbled across the prairies. At night the lights from the campfires flickered and etched the faces of men and women and children. Dawn and the ox-whip cracked. The frontier rolled. They needed a firearm to hunt and a firearm to protect them against the Indian. History set the rods for Colt lightening to strike.

The wave of migration to California was different from the other western treks. The others sought a home. This rush was for gold and quick riches and brought the adventurer and the criminal as well as the industrious citizen. The bowie knife and the revolver was the law and order.

Major Cross wrote, "While on a march to the Columbia River, I considered Colt's six-shooter as an invaluable weapon on the western prairies, where you frequently meet hostile bands of Indians. While on this long march, when hunting or running buffalo, I seldom ever saw any other pistol used. The Colt repeating pistol was much sought after by the emigrants and sold in Oregon at from sixty to eighty dollars."

The frontier accepted the Colt because the weapon was needed to win the West. "Express-riders that carry the mails through the Indian country always make it a condition that they should be furnished with Colt's revolvers; otherwise they would not risk their lives in such service," wrote Captain French.

Other states were carved or born.
Texas grew from hide and horn.

Man and horse and Colt revolver became one in the great plains of Texas. The Comanche Indian had made the mounted Texas Ranger and equipped him with the Colt because the Comanche Indian was a dangerous warrior and better equipped than the white adversary. From his racing horse, the Comanche could carry one hundred arrows and shoot them so rapidly as to keep one or more in the air all the time and each with sufficient force to drive the shaft entirely through the buffalo body. The Comanches also were artists in the use of the lance. The Texas Ranger had a single shot pistol. He could carry two pistols at the most in addition to his single-shot rifle. The total of the two pistols and rifle combined was three shots and a minute each to reload. This was the wide-open spaces where the Ranger was completely exposed. No woods, forest or glades could shield him. He must be an excellent marksman and an excellent horseman. "There is but one weapon, the six-shooter when properly handled, is the only weapon," wrote Texas Ranger "Rip" Ford. The mounted Texas Ranger needed horizon and power. The horse elevated him to conquer space and the Colt enlarged his sphere of influence to conquer danger.

In the Fall of 1855 Colt completed his Armory in Hartford, Connecticut, the largest arms plant in the world and employed about 900 people. The factory system was comparatively new and had brought much misery. Colt introduced recreational facilities for employees. He built Charter Oak Hall, a combination of Assembly hall with recreation and reading rooms. He brought lecturers, music, theatricals and encouraged debating. He used a system of contracting but set up a minimum scale. He pioneered in the establishment of old age pensions.

For his Armory Colt had bought 500 acres in the South Meadow section of Hartford that had Connecticut River frontage. The river would rise out of banks nearly every Spring and flood half of South Meadow. Samuel Colt built dikes and bound them with protective willows in imitation of Holland. The gray willows flourished. An inquiry about the price of the willow crop came one day from a furniture manufacturer who imported willow from abroad. This set Colt to investigate. A market for willow furniture existed but skilled workers were at a premium. Colt wrote C. F. Wappenhans, his agent in Germany to recruit some willow workers. It was an impossible assignment, replied Wappenhans, because the willow workers were generally engaged in a cooperative project of making willow furniture a particular, hamlet with many ties of family and friends. Wappenhans illustrated his point with the example of a particular willow manufacturing hamlet near Potsdam in Germany. It was moulded in a pattern of life and living and was not interested in coming to Hartford. Colt offered to reproduce the entire hamlet in Hartford exactly as it was in Potsdam. They agreed. Wappenhans sent detailed plans of their homes, their beer garden, the bandstand, and described their food, their customs, the musical instruments, the music, all down to the most minute detail.

Colt fulfilled the bargain. In the Southeast corner of his reclaimed land he built a copy of their hamlet with its Swiss architecture, and they came. They split, peeled and wove the willow, by hand. Colt invented a machine to split and peel the willow. It could split and peel willow quicker and cleaner than done by hand. Soon "Colt Willow-Ware Works" dominated the willow furniture market; wares grew in variety,— chandeliers, picture frames, chains, invalid chairs; and the sales were pushed to Cuba and South America. The band played at all his functions.

To the reproduced quaint communty, Colt had added his philosophy that there can be no economy where there is no efficiency and there can be no efficiency where there is no machinery.

On June 5, 1856, Samuel Colt was married to Elizabeth Hart Jarvis and took his bride on a honeymoon trip to Europe to attend the coronation of the Russian Emperor Alexander 2nd. As a private citizen of the United States, Colt was not entitled to witness the coronation so he received an appointment as a special attache to the American Embassy to Russia.

Colt heard of Louis Kossuth and General Garibaldi's appeal for freedom and independence of their respective countries, Kossuth for Hungary, Garibaldi for Italy, both under Austrian domination. To

Kossuth he sent a presentation set and an invitation to visit his London factory. Kossuth replied, "I dare hope soon to have occasion to use it, and use it, and use it I shall with the conscientious conviction that your genius never could have aided a better cause." Colt sent Garibaldi a contribution of arms for his cause. Garibaldi replied, "The arrival of your arms will be hailed among us, not merely as material aid dispatched by a man of heart to a people who fight for their most sacred rights, but as a subsidy of moral potency from the great American nation." Surely they would need arms for their objectives. Was his ear attuned to opportunity or was it sympathy for freedom stirring?

Colt offered his services to the newly inaugurated President Abraham Lincoln as the war began and he commenced to enlarge his plant. On January 10, 1862, Samuel Colt died, not yet 48 years of age and left an estate of over five million dollars.

Modern biography seeks to explain the personality of Samuel Colt by the revelation of the unconscious springs of action. The psychiatrist that would attempt to help us with an explanation as what made Sammy run asks, "Do you know anything of what happened to him before the age of three?" We do not know that but we do know the achievements of Sammy's running. That must suffice. Therefore we present him from one angle of vision. We do not have the gift to view him with a vision of 360 degrees. Only in relation to the labyrinth of his time and tradition do we study Samuel Colt.

Basic forces of history made the Colt revolver a success. The Mexican War emphasized the need for the Colt six shooters. The Texas plainsman had already realized its value. Battering expansion followed, of ramming through the West, the Mormons, the Gold Rush, Kansas, Know-Nothing Party—all followed in rapid succession and they all wanted a practical firearm. Colt had the answer.

Colt's life span was the percussion period of ignition in firearms. His invention translated percussion into a practical system and into a mass produced revolver.

Colt cooperated with the basic forces because of his genius for penetration into an understanding of the opportunity. We cannot heap history upon the premise of determinism. We have our decisive freedoms. What we do with them depends on our awareness of them. Samuel Colt saw the possibilities and grasped them. Therefore the mantle of selection fell on his shoulders.

The cynic may say that these fortuitous circumstances combined to make the Colt a successful invention. Time and chance happened to Colt. The cynic must remember that it was Colt's method of advertising, far in advance of his day, that proclaimed the testimonials. Possessed by the fervor of the evangelist of an electric energy, not of nerves, but of will, he pushed onward. It may be that he found release for his loneliness in evangelism. It may be related to his frustrated childhood that lacked the love and affection of a mother. Whatever the cause, the symptoms of an intense drive was there. Colt was shrewd and able. He had an awareness of the opportunity and grasped at it with all his might. He had a pleasant personality, loved and understood people. He moved in many circles and was at ease in all. His enthusiasm struck fire. Approbation could not deceive him nor criticism dishearten him. He had a stout heart. External circumstances did not affect him externally, but brought suffering to his sensitive inner self. The ideals by which we live, the standards by which we set the meaning of our lives is also an invention.

Colt was cast down by the critics. They that sat at the altar of the sacred cow chased him from their precious precincts. He was a violator, he had a new idol, first misunderstood, later feared, then jealous, but at each turn they were iconoclasts. They could not destroy his idol because it was spun of dreams.

CHAPTER TWO

ROTATING CHAMBERED-BREECH FIREARMS
By SAMUEL COLT

The London Institute of Civil Engineers, a society incorporated in 1828 and before whom Samuel Colt read the following paper, November 25, 1851, and was thereupon elected their first American member and received the Telford medal.

INSTITUTION OF CIVIL ENGINEERS
November 25, 1851
SIR WILLIAM CUBITT, President, in the Chair

No. 862.—"On the application of Machinery to the manufacture of Rotating Chambered-Breech Fire-Arms, and the peculiarities of those Arms."* By COLONEL SAMUEL COLT (U. S. America), Assoc. Inst. C. E.†

AMONG the various departments of practical science, there is perhaps none in which more rapid advancement has been made within the present century, than in the manufacture of firearms, and great ingenuity has been displayed in devising improvements in them; but it is the extent to which machinery may be used in their construction, that must render the subject interesting to Engineers.

It is not the design of this paper, to enter upon a history of the first employment of firearms, nor yet to trace all the graduations of improvement that have taken place, since their introduction as weapons of war, such a subject being somewhat foreign to the scientific views, and peaceful occupations of Civil Engineers; but as experience has shown, that perfect weapons of defence are indispensable for the pioneers of civilization in new countries, and still as necessary for the preservation of peace in old countries, the best means of producing them by the aid of machinery, must be interesting; it is therefore intended, briefly to examine, chronologically, as far as recent researches extend, the gradual advances in the form and construction of firearms with magazines, or chambers, for repeated discharges, and to contrast them with the modern repeating chambered-breech arms introduced by the Author.

The principal collections of arms examined for this purpose are those in the Tower of London, the United Service Museum, the Rotunda at Woolwich, Warwick Castle, in England, and the Musee d'Artillerie, and the

---

* The discussion upon this subject was extended over a portion of two evenings, but an abstract of the whole is given consecutively.

† The Author was subsequently elected Assoc. Inst. C. E. May 4, 1852.

Hotel Cluny, at Paris; all these show that at all times and in all countries, the attention of armourers has been constantly directed to the subject, and much ingenuity has been displayed in the improvement of these engines of destruction, and as the use of gunpowder became better understood, and firearms were more generally employed, the desire to improve them increased, and their construction was materially changed. The chief progressive steps, after their first introduction, were, the hand-gun, the match-lock, the pyrites, or wheel-lock, the flint-lock, and the percussion lock.*

The Author had been aware since the year 1835, of the existence of ancient examples of repeating firearms, but it has only been on the occasion of his present visit to Europe in 1851, that he has been able to devote any attention to their chronological history, as exhibited in the specimens, existing in the museums, and private collections, to which he has recently obtained access. These specimens it is necessary to describe briefly, in order to render apparent the simplicity of design, the superiority of workmanship, the uniformity of construction by means of machinery, and the thorough efficiency of the repeating arms now submitted to the Institution.

The earliest specimen, which the Author has been enabled to discover, is a match-lock gun now in the Armoury of the Tower of London, supposed to be of the fifteenth century, (Fig. 1, Plate 1). It has a revolving breech with four chambers, mounted on an arbor parallel with, and welded to the barrel. The hinder end of the arbor is attached to the gunstock, by a transverse pin, or nail. Notches are made in a flange, at the fore end of the breech, to receive the end of a spring, fixed to the stock, and extending across the breech, for the purpose of locking it, when a chamber is brought up into a line with the barrel. The antiquity of this arm is evident, from the match-lock contrivance for igniting the charge, and the fittings, and mounting indicate an Eastern origin. Each charge chamber is provided with a priming pan, with a swing cover, which, before firing, would require to be pushed aside by the finger, to present the priming powder to the match. A repetition of the fire is effected by throwing back the match-holder, and turning the breech by hand, to bring up another loaded chamber.

In the collection at the Musee d'Artillerie, at Paris, there are two specimens of match-lock guns, with revolving breeches, both of them being very similar to that which has been described; these have each eight chambers rotating by hand, and the covers of the priming magazines require to be pushed back by the finger before firing.

The next match-lock arm (Fig. 2, Plate 1,) was found, by the Author, in the possession of Messrs. Forsyth and Co., who obtained it, about twenty-

---

* The first small fire-arms were called Hand Cannons and were fired from a rest, by the application of a match; when their weight was further reduced and a match-lock was added, they called Calivers. In a short time they were mounted on a stock, rendered more portable, and termed Arquebuse; the shorter arms of this kind being called Petronel, or Poitrinal, from their being fired from the shoulder, without a rest. The German Reiters introduced the Pistol, named from Pistoia, in Etruria, a place celebrated for the manufacture of that species of arms. The introduction of the Musket, the Rifle, and the various modifications of them, has been very gradual, but has been accelerated latterly, by the general determination to give long-range arms to the troops.—

Sec. Inst. C.E.

four years ago, from the late Lord William Bentinck, the Governor-General of India, whence it was brought, with other curious weapons. The construction of this arm closely resembles that shown in Fig. 1, just described; but the workmanship is superior, and it is more elaborately ornamented. The breech, which requires to be moved by hand, has five chambers, each having a priming pan with a swing cover. The arbor is attached to the barrel, which, at the end adjoining the breech, is enlarged to correspond with the diameter of the revolving chamber, to which it forms a kind of shield.

But in order to mitigate the danger, which was, no doubt, apprehended, from the simultaneous discharge of all the chambers, by the spreading of the fire, from the exploding chamber, which would be the inevitable effect of this shield, the maker has provided vents for the charges, by boring holes through the enlargement of the barrel, corresponding to the charge chambers in the revolving breech. In one respect this gun gives evidence of progress, inasmuch as the breech-arbor is more firmly secured to the stock by two square pins, thus ensuring a firmer connexion between the parts. The method of locking the breech is similar to that of the first arm described (Fig. 1), except, that the spring for securing the breech is fastened to the barrel instead of to the stock. The thinness of the metal of the barrels and the extreme length of the revolving chambers, in both these specimens of arms, would seem to indicate the bad quality of the gunpowder used at the period of the irconstruction.

The third specimen is a decided advance on the preceding guns. This arm (Fig. 3, Plate 1,), which was found in the Armoury at the Tower, is furnished with a Pyrites wheel lock, and one priming pan is common to all the six chambers of the revolving breech; this pan is fitted with a sliding cover, and is so arranged that the serrated edge of a vertical wheel may project into it, amongst the loose powder in the pan; to this wheel a rapid rotary motion is given, by means of a trigger spring, acting upon a link lever, attached to the arbor of the wheel, the teeth of which, striking upon the pyrites, create the sparks which ignite the priming powder. The fire is then communicated laterally to a train of powder about 2½ inches long, before it reaches the charge in the breech, and which train of powder and priming require to be renewed, each time, before the charge in the adjoining chambers can be exploded. A stop-pin is made to enter the orifices in the wheel, to stay its action, until the proper time, and on pulling the trigger the firing is effected.

In this instance, also, the breech is rotated by hand, and the barrel and breech are brought into contact, by a nut working upon the threaded end of the breech arbor. By the employment of one priming pan for all the chambers, and from the apparent necessity for closing the rear end of the breech with a cap, so as to leave but one small opening for the passage of the fire, from the priming-pan to the breech, the liability of the several chambers to be simultaneously fired was greatly increased; for the cap, which covers the rear end of the breech, prevents the escape of the fire laterally, and forms, in fact, a channel for guiding the deflected fire to the touch-holes of all the charges. This gun has no stock in front of the breech; but, unlike the previous specimens, the barrel is cut away on each side, so as to allow the balls to escape, in case of premature explosion. A pistol of nearly identical construction (Fig. 4, Plate 1) is in the collection at the Rotunda, at Woolwich.

In the Hotel Cluny at Paris, there is an arm of the 17th century, with a pyrites lock, and eight chambers, very similar in general construction to that found in the Tower, but differing materially in the arrangement of the touch-holes. There is one main priming tube, extending from the pan to the rear of the revolving chambers, with eight corresponding tubes, extending from the rear, to within a short distance of the front end, where an orifice is pierced into each chamber, for the purpose of igniting the charge immediately behind the bullet; thus obliging the charge to burn backwards, towards the breech. This arrangement, which was evidently made for the purpose of preventing the simultaneous explosion of the charges, has produced a construction of arm, almost identical with that of the modern Prussian needle gun, for which the great feature of the more rapid ignition of the whole of the charge of powder has been claimed. The priming-tube, and the pan, as in the arm at the Tower, require to be filled with gunpowder every time a chamber is discharged.

Fig. 5, Plate 1, represents an elaborately finished Spanish gun of a more recent date, with a flint lock. The breech is rotated by hand, and it is locked in the proper position for firing, by a pin, which enters a hole in the rear end of the breech, and which has to be drawn back, prior to bringing up a fresh chamber in a line with the barrel. The chief peculiarity of this gun is, that a magazine of priming powder is provided, immediately above a fixed priming pan, which serves for the four chambers of the breech. The magazine is hinged to the pan and is fitted with a sliding bottom, which when drawn out, is intended to allow a certain amount of powder to fall into the pan, and when pushed back cuts off the supply. The rear surface of this magazine serves also as the steel, or striking surface for the hammer, and it is ribbed on its face to receive the blow of the descending flint. The fore end of the breech is closed in by a filling piece of wood, attached to the barrel, and the hinder end is enclosed in a cap, as in the last example. This arm is therefore like the others fatally defective, the priming powder in the magazine would inevitably explode; the priming fire would be conducted to all the other touch-holes, and the lateral fire, at the other end of the breech, would be directed into the several chambers, and explode all the charges prematurely.

In the Armoury at Warwick Castle there is a gun which appears to be an attempt to insure greater safety in firing, but at the expense of greater complexity of mechanism. It has a flint lock and a breech with four chambers, to be rotated by hand; each chamber is furnished with a priming-pan, and a steel, which latter forms also the cover. The firing of one charge is not, therefore, so liable to ignite the powder in the other chambers. The stock in front of the breech is very thin, so as not to cover the other three chambers; consequently, if a premature explosion took place, no material injury could occur to the arm. The chambers would appear to have been fastened by a spring from the end of the barrel.

An arm very similar in construction to the last was found in the Tower of London (Fig. 6, Plate 1). The breech is composed of four distinct tubes, or chambers, attached together by two end plates. Each tube, or chamber, is provided with a priming-pan and steel, and the breech is rotated by hand. It is retained in the required position for firing, by a bolt acting upon the rear end, which is withdrawn, by hand, when the breech is required to be moved round on its arbor.

The specimen (Fig. 7, Plate 1), which appears from its construction, to come next in order of date, was obtained by the Author from Messrs. Forsyth and Co.; it bears the evidence of English construction, as on the lock is inscribed "John Dafte, London," in characters which indicate that it is scarcely more than a century old; it may, however, be a copy of an older arm. There is evidently an attempt, in this arm, to produce a more compact weapon, for instead of having a projecting pan and steel for each chamber, recesses are made in the periphery of the breech, to form pans, and one steel was probably provided to stand over the breech, attached to the barrel. The breech, containing six chambers, is rotated by hand, and is locked when in position for firing, in the same manner as in Fig. 3; priming powder is also placed in a pan for each chamber, whilst the weapon is being loaded; these priming pans are each covered by a sliding plate working in parallel guides affixed to the periphery of the breech, with the intention of protecting, in a more perfect manner, the priming of the adjoining chambers, and thus preventing premature explosion. Connected with the hammer, is a small bar which projects forward, so that when the trigger is pulled, the hammer, in its descent against the steel, brings the small bar into contact with a projection on the cover of the upper priming pan, pushing it forward, and exposing the powder in the pan to the action of the sparks struck from the flint of the hammer. This arrangement has the advantage of compactness, and in this particular it may be considered a mechanical improvement on its predecessors; the stock does not reach beyond the base of the breech, and the barrel is cut out in front of the chambers, to allow the balls to escape, in case of premature explosion. This arm bears evidence of being radically defective; for in consequence of the holder of the steel being fastened over one of the chambers, into which the fire would be deflected, premature explosion necessarily followed, the steel was broken off and the arm was probably rendered useless by the first discharge.

In the collection at the United Service Museum, London, is a brass model pistol, with six chambers, said to have been constructed in the time of Charles the First. This specimen displays more ingenuity and greater skill, in its design, than any of the early weapons hitherto discovered; but it is, evidently, only a model of a proposed construction, and has never been practically tested, as if it had been used, it would have been blown to pieces by the first discharge. In its general design it greatly resembles the arm last described; each chamber being provided with a similar priming pan and sliding plate to cover it, and attached to the hammer is a bar, for pushing back the cover, and exposing the powder to the fire from the flint. A steel, for the flint to strike on, is jointed to the barrel, in the same place and in the same manner as in the arm, Fig. 7, Plate 1, and is consequently open to the same objections. The arbor, on which the breech turns, is screwed into the barrel and is attached to the stock by a pin passing through it. From this description, it will be understood, that the model under consideration is tolerably free from the defects previously pointed out; but inasmuch as it possesses no means of regulating the contact of the breech and the barrel, so as to prevent the spread of lateral fire, it, like all the preceding specimens, offers no security against the simultaneous discharge of all the chambers.

It is not a little surprising, that the next example of a rotating chambered-breech gun, with a flint lock, Fig. 8, Plate 1, patented by Elisha H. Collier (U.S. America), in 1818, should exhibit nearly all the serious defects which had doubtless been discovered, and had been, to some extent, remedied by the earlier makers. The objectionable parts of this arm are the priming magazine, the flue which would conduct the fire round to the different touch-holes, and the cap in front, which would direct the lateral fire into the adjoining chambers. The breech is made to bear against the barrel, by means of a coiled spring, which would probably be efficient while the gun was clean, and each chamber is recessed to receive the abutting end of the barrel, with the intention of effecting a closer junction. This bearing up of the chambered-breech against the barrel is maintained, during the firing, by a bolt which is thrust forward by a cam on the spindle of the hammer, when the trigger is pulled, and would be effective for a few discharges, until the junction between the cylinder and the barrel, or the arbor on which the cylinder turns, became foul. The valve, which forms the bottom of the priming magazine, is self-acting and supplies a certain quantity of powder to the pan, when the magazine (which forms at the same time the cover of the pan, and the steel for the hammer to strike upon), is brought into its elevated position. In order to rotate the breech, the hammer is thrown back to half-cock, the breech is then drawn out of contact with the barrel, and another chamber may be turned up by hand into a line with it.

The arrangement of the flint-lock chambered-breech firearm, contrived by Wheeler of Boston, and patented by Cornelius Coolidge, in August, 1819,* differs from the arm patented by E. H. Collier (in whose patents Coolidge was interested), in having fastened to the chamber, and to the arbor, a coiled, or spiral spring, which being wound up, is intended to constitute a power for assisting in causing the cylinder chambers to rotate, as by a complicated arrangement in the lock, an escapement motion was effected by the action of the lock itself. This arm possesses all the complication, and the imperfections of the worst of the other arms, with the same liability to premature explosion, and these defects have been admitted, inasmuch as E. H. Collier acknowledged that "in manufacturing these arms he improved the gun as he went on, and left out the spring because he thought it was useless,"—"he wanted to get rid of all superfluous parts, and left the spring out, because he considered the gun was better without it;" thus leaving the chambered-breech to be rotated by hand.

During the latter part of the last century many ingenious persons directed their attention to the improvement of firearms, with a view to simplify their

---

* Vide "Description des Machines et Procedes specifies dans les Brevets, d'invention, de perfectionnement et d'importation." Tome xi, page 42, Paris, 1825.

construction, to render them more effective, and to combine safety with celerity in firing.

Among some of the most important of these improvements, may be mentioned, the peculiarly constructed breech, patented by Mr. Henry Nock, in 1787, and the application of fulminating powder for igniting the charge in the chamber of the barrel, for which the Rev. Mr. Forsyth obtained a patent in 1807; the principal objects of this latter invention were to supersede the flint lock, and to obtain the rapid and complete combustion of the whole charge in the barrel, so as to obviate the loss of force which formerly resulted from the escape of air through the touch-hole. Many ingenious contrivances have since been introduced by the manufacturers of firearms, of different countries, for simplifying the mechanical arrangement for firing by percussion, the adoption of which has now become general.

These improvements advanced firearms towards perfection; but still they laboured under great disadvantages, chiefly from the waste of time in reloading, which prevented the full extent of the rapidity of discharge, that an ordinary gun constructed of iron and steel could endure, from being taken advantage of.

The Author, living in a country of most extensive frontier, still inhabited by hordes of aborigines, and knowing the insulated position of the enterprising pioneer, and his dependence, sometimes alone, on his personal ability to protect himself and family, had often meditated upon the inefficiency of the ordinary double-barrelled gun and pistol, both involving a loss of time in reloading, which was too frequently fatal, in the peculiar character of Indian border warfare.

By the United States' Government, also, it was considered an object of great importance, to obtain an effective repeating arm, as the peculiar characteristic of the mode of attack by the mounted Indians, was to overwhelm small bodies of American soldiers, by rushing down on them, in greatly superior numbers, after having drawn their fire, and then to despatch them, whilst in a comparatively defenceless state, from the necessity of reloading their arms.

After much reflection and repeated trials, he effected an arrangement in the construction of revolving firearms, without having seen, or being aware, at that period (1829) of any arm more effective than a double-barrelled gun having ever been constructed, and it was only during a visit to Europe, in the year 1835, that he discovered he was not the first person who had conceived the idea of repeating firearms, with a rotating chambered-breech.

The first arrangement, contrived by the Author, was the combination of a number of long barrels, to rotate upon a spindle, by the act of cocking the lock, and similar in construction to those now generally made; but from the weight and bulk of the arm, it soon appeared better to have only a rotating cylinder containing several chambers, and to discharge through one barrel. For this he took out a patent in 1835, in which he claimed as peculiarly his own, the arrangement, or construction shown in Figs. 9 and 10.

Fig. 9, Plate 1, represents a pistol, exhibiting the mechanical combination of the arm at that early stage; the hammer is hung at the fulcrum A: the key bolt, or catch lever which holds the cylinder, is hung at the fulcrum B. The lifter, to move the ratchet, has a working connection with the hammer on the left side, at C. The arm, D, of the lifter, works into the teeth of the ratchet, on the left: E, represents the ratchet, when connected with the shackle. F, F, is the middle and forward part of the shackle, on which the ratchet is placed. G, is the arbor on which the cylinder revolves: the end H, is the nut that holds the arbor in its place, when in the shield: I, I, represent the forward end of the arbor, which passes through the plate, and the projection on the lower part of the barrel, and the barrel is secured to the arbor by a key at J. K, represents the fulcrum of the trigger: L, is the spring which forces the connecting rod against the end of the hammer: M, is the spring which forces the key that holds the cylinder: O, is the main spring. By drawing back the hammer, the pin P, operates upon the after end of the key-bolt, or catch-lever, that locks the cylinder and raises it, consequently, the other end R, is drawn from the cylinder, and the arm D, of the lifter begins to act on a tooth S, on the left side of the ratchet, which being connected with the cylinder, by means of the shackle, turns until the next chamber is brought opposite the barrel. When the pin P, is relieved from the key, by passing over its upper end T, the pin allows the end R, of the key, to be forced by means of the spring M, into the succeeding ward of the cylinder: at the same time, by the action of the lower end of the hammer U, upon the connecting rod V, a forward horizontal motion of the rod is produced, when the end W, is brought in contact with the upper projection of the trigger, and forces it down to a proper position for the finger, when the claw X, of the trigger, hooks into the connecting rod, which holds the hammer, when drawn back, or set, by means of the end V, entering the lower catch Y, on the hammer.

On pulling the trigger to discharge the pistol, the connecting rod is drawn from the catch of the hammer, when the main spring forces the hammer forward, the upper end striking the percussion cap; during which operation the lifter, by means of its lateral motion to the left, falls below a succeeding tooth on the ratchet: when by the lateral motion of the after end Q of the key, which holds the cylinder, the pin P, of the hammer, is permitted again to fall below it. By repetitions of the same motion of the hammer, the same effect is produced until each succeeding chamber is brought round and is discharged.

Fig. 10, Plate 1, represents the principle of the invention as applicable to rifles and muskets. In order to set the lock, the fulcrum of the lever being at A, by drawing down the ring B, the end C, operates upon the rod D, of the hammer, whose fulcrum being at E, throws back its end F, when the trigger at G, whose fulcrum is at H, operates upon the catches of the hammer, at I, to hold the lock when it is set. When the end F, of the hammer, is removed from the adopter, whose bearings are at J, J, it is drawn back by means of the coiled spring K, until its end L, is drawn back sufficiently to allow the cylinder to turn. After the finger is released from the lever, when the lock is set, a small spring draws it back to its former place, to make room for the end D, of the hammer, so that its force may not be impaired. By pulling the trigger from the catch of the hammer, the main spring, which is connected to the hammer by the stirrup O, forces its end F, forward against the end M, of the adopter, whose end L, is brought in contact with the percussion cap, placed upon the tube N, so as to explode the charge of powder. In loading the arm it is only requisite to draw the key J, which will liberate the barrel; then by drawing the key that locks the cylinder, which is effected by drawing back the hammer to half-cock, the cylinder may be taken from the arbor.

Fig. 11, Plate 1, represents a rifle made by the Author, in 1836, to rotate and fire by the continued action of the lever, or by the use of a trigger.

The arms so constructed, consisting of a large number of pieces, and assembled in a complicated manner, were soon found to possess many practical disadvantages, arising chiefly from the wish of the Author to construct compact and good-looking weapons. His original experiments had all been made on skeleton arms, solely with a view to utility, and in them there was not the liability to premature explosion, from the escape of fire at the mouth of the chamber, or by the inter-communication of the ignited detonating caps; but when he enclosed the rear, and the mouths of the rotating chambers, the fire, being confined beneath the shield and the cap, was communicated successively to the percussion caps, and in front was conveyed into the chambers, so that premature and simultaneous explosion of the charges necessarily took place.

In consequence of these premature explosions, it became necessary to remove the shield, from over the base of the chambers, and to introduce partitions, between the nipples, or cones, to prevent the fire from spreading to and exploding the adjoining caps; but this only partially accomplished the object. There still remained risk of explosion from the spreading of the fire laterally between the base of the barrel and the face of the chamber. To meet this danger, the metal plate which was attached to the barrel, and projected over the chambers, was removed; this obviated to a certain extent, but did not altogether prevent, the simultaneous explosion of the charges; for during a trial of the arm, by order of the American Government[*] an accident occurred, from the simultaneous explosion of two chambers, which induced the Author, after much reflection, to give a slight chamfer, or bevil to the orifice of each chamber, so as to deflect, or throw off at an outward angle, the fire which expanded laterally across their mouths. The reason for this alteration was, that when the lateral fire met the rectangular edge of the orifice of the chambers, the angle of incidence being equal to the angle of reflection, the fire was conducted downwards, or inwards to the charge; but when the flame struck the chamfered edge, it was directed outwards away from the charge. This action is shown in wood-cut (Fig. 1), and unimportant as this alteration may appear, it has proved so effectual, that if loose powder is placed over the charge, in the adjoining chambers, it is not now ignited when the pistol is discharged. These and other improvements have brought the firearm to its present safe and effective condition, and the Author believes, that no casualty can occur, nor that more than one charge can be fired at one time, if the metal is sound and the arm is properly loaded.

---

[*] Vide "Report of the Secretary of War, 25th Congress, First Session, June 1837."

Fig. 1

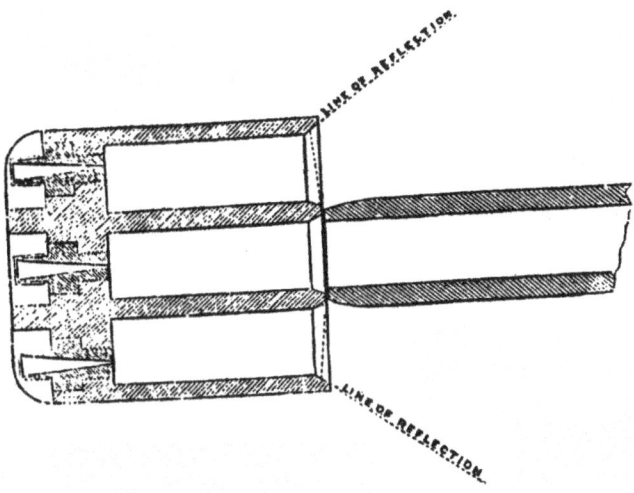

The early arms of the Author were made from 1836 to 1842, partly by hand labour, and partly by machinery, by the Patent Arms' Company, established at Paterson, United States, where a capital of nearly £30,000 was expended without any beneficial result, except in gaining experience, both in the arms themselves and in the machinery required for their manufacture.

About the year 1837 the Florida war broke out, when the Seminole Indians, retreating into the "everglades," defied the power of the United States troops, and a comparative handful of savages resisted successfully, for a long time, all the forces sent against them. The Indians were as expert in the use of the rifle as their white invaders, who could make little, or no impression on them; in this strait the Government applied to the Author, who went to the seat of war with a supply of repeating arms, which even in their then comparatively rude state were found so effective, that more were ordered, and in the hands of the hardy-mounted Rangers, commanded by General Harney, who by their aid became the terror of the Red men, the war was soon brought to an end, for when the Indians saw their foes fire six times without lowering their weapons to load, they knew their former tactics were useless and they surrendered. This success, however, though very glorious for the Government, was exactly the reverse for the Author, for by exterminating the Indians and bringing the war rapidly to an end, the market for the arms was destroyed. They were, however, most successfully used by Commodore Moore, of the Texas Navy, as well as by Colonel Jack Hays and other distinguished Texan Rangers, during the wars with Mexico and the Indians from 1837 to 1848.

In consequence of the peace they were scarcely again employed, until the year 1847, when the Mexican campaign commenced, under the command of General Taylor, who having seen the utility of these weapons in Florida, where he was also in command, sent Captain Walker, of the Texan Rangers, to procure from the Author a supply of these arms; not one however could be procured, but by great exertion, commensurate with the exigencies of the period, a number were manufactured, and it has been stated that "those Texan Rangers, with Colt's repeaters, walked right into the towns and hamlets of the Mexicans and drove the population out against all resistance."

Colonel Charles A. May, the celebrated dragoon officer in giving evidence respecting the arms said, "These arms were used with a great deal of effect, by General Harney, during the Seminole war; since then I have had them almost constantly; and at the commencement of the Mexican war, was fortunate in procuring some of them; by General Taylor's order I armed one of my squadrons with them, and found them very useful. When I went last into New Mexico, I armed all my force with them. They were used with great effect. They possess very many advantages over the ordinary arms. They have great precision, and are shot with great facility, accuracy, and force. They are much more efficient than the ordinary arms. They can be used very readily while on horseback, while at full speed, with great accuracy. I have found no difficulty in shooting a ball through a buffalo. I do not know whether the Texan Rangers in the Mexican war were armed with these pistols by the Government, but almost every one had them. They were very much dreaded by the Mexicans. The Texans use them with great precision. I have no hesitation in saying, that I consider that ten men with Colt's pistols in their belts, and who understand their use, can go anywhere, and can keep off almost any force. I should not hesitate, with ten men, armed with these pistols, to go anywhere across the plains."

Such is the general history of the weapon, and in the manufacture, numerous improvements naturally suggested themselves, both in the arms and in the tools used in their production, until the former assumed their present shape, and the latter almost entirely superseded hand labour.

Figs. 12, 13, and 14, Plate 1, represent the arms as at present constructed, at the Author's manufactory, at Hartford, Connecticut, U. S. America. They differ from those formerly made, principally in the greater simplicity and the better proportions of the parts of the lock and the framework; important additions and improvements have been made in the loading lever, and rammer for forcing the balls firmly into the cylinder, (Fig. 12, Plate 1), the employment of the helical, or spiral groove on the arbor, on which the cylinder turns, whose sharp edges are intended to prevent fouling, by scraping off any smoke, or dirt accumulating on the cylinder, from the lateral fire entering the centre opening; and the inclined plane leading to the recesses on the periphery of the cylinder, to direct the bolt below the opposite shoulder in the recesses; thus preventing the cylinder from being accidentally thrown too far, by the sudden action of cocking. The lock (as shown by Fig 15, Plate 1, which is a skeleton arm, expressly arranged to exhibit the working parts,) is now composed of five working parts, instead of seventeen, as formerly, and it is obvious, that if the several parts of the machinery are made proportionally strong, for the work they have to do, so is the arm rendered more efficient by the greater simplicity of the general construction.

In all arms having a moveable breech, it is desirable to bring the barrel and cylinder as nearly in contact as possible, in order to prevent the escape of lateral fire, and yet to leave freedom for motion, without friction; this is now effected by the base pin, on which the cylinder turns, entering a corresponding opening in the under part of the barrel, being there held in place by a key, passing through and bearing against the back end of the slot in the barrel, and the fore end of the slot in the base pin, which is thus drawn up to the bottom of the hole, and yet the barrel is prevented from being brought too close upon, or in absolute contact with, the cylinder, whilst its end is still held in its proper position with respect to the cylinder. In the event of any abrasion of the end of the cylinder, or of the barrel, by deepening the cavity, or filing the end of the base pin, the key can be driven further in, and the proper distance for the readjustment of those parts be maintained, whilst the essential rigidity of structure is secured.

In loading the present arm, it is necessary to draw back the hammer to the half notch, to allow the cylinder to be rotated freely by hand; a charge of powder is then placed in each chamber, and the balls, without wadding, or patch, are put one at a time upon the mouths of the chambers, turned under the rammer and forced down, by the lever, below the mouth of the chamber. This is repeated until all the chambers are loaded. Percussion caps are then placed on the nipples, when by drawing back the hammer to the full catch, the click, or lever is brought into contact with one of the ratchet teeth, on the base of the cylinder, bringing the nipple into the precise position to receive the blow of the hammer; the arm is then in a condition for being discharged by simply pulling the trigger; and a repetition of the same motion produces the like results, until all the chambers are discharged through the barrel.

Machinery is now employed by the Author, to the extent of about eight tenths of the whole cost of construction of these firearms; he was induced gradually to use machinery to so great an extent, by finding that with hand labour it was not possible to obtain that amount of uniformity, or accuracy in the several parts, which is so desirable, and also because he could not otherwise get the number of arms made, at anything like the same cost, as by machinery. Thus he obtains uniformity as well as cheapness in the production of the various parts, and when a new piece is required, a duplicate can be supplied with greater accuracy and less expense, than could be done by the most skilful manual labour, or on active service a number of complete arms may be readily made up from portions of broken ones, picked up after an action.

To minutely describe and illustrate the machinery would absorb too much time, and render this paper to voluminous, there being hundreds of distinct operations, involving a great variety of peculiar contrivances and mechanical motions; a general description of the mode in which the various parts of the arm are manufactured, will suffice to render the system clear to engineers, conversant with the effect of machines; and the specimens (placed on the table), which are entirely formed by machinery, will illustrate the description.

The manufacture of arms, both in Great Britain and on the Continent, is carried on almost entirely by manual labour, the various parts being forged, filed and ground into the requisite form, by workmen at their own houses, the barrels alone being forged, bored, and ground, in manufactories established for the purpose, and machinery being employed only for cutting out the stocks. At the Government small arms manufactory, at Enfield, under the intelligent direction of Mr. Lovell, steps onward have, however, been made, in the use of machinery for some portions of the work. Still no general uniformity among the parts can exist, and in America, where manual labor is both scarce and expensive, it was imperative to devise means for producing these arms with the greatest rapidity and economy, and at the same time with such uniform precision, as could only result from the use of self-acting tools.

The machinery requisite for constructing the repeating firearms, though at first view, like a cotton, or silk factory, apparently intricate, is in reality composed of the simplest elements, and consists in a repetition of known mechanical actions specially applied. It will suffice to describe the operations on a few parts, commencing with the lock frame, which is the basis of the hole, and to which all the other parts are adapted.

Like all the other parts, the lock frame is forged by swages, and its shape completed by one blow. The action of the machines commences by fixing the centre, and drilling and tapping the base for receiving the arbor, which having been previously prepared,—the helical groove cut on it, and the lower end screwed,—is firmly fixed into its position, furnishing a definite point from which all the operations are performed and to which all the parts bear relation. The facing and hollowing of the recoil shield and frame; the cutting and sinking the central recesses; the cutting out all the grooves and orifices, planing the several flat surfaces, and shaping the curved parts, prepare the frame for being introduced between hard steel clamps, through which all the holes are drilled, bored and tapped, for the various screws; so that after passing through twenty-two distinct operations, the lock frame is ready for finishing by hand, which consists in merely removing the rough edge, or burr, left by the machinery, and giving it the last polish and hardening.

The rotating chambered cylinder is forged from a solid piece of steel, turned, channelled, tapped, polished, and engraved, and then the chambers are bored out by a machine, which insures the most perfect precision of dimensions and uniformity of relative position.

In the same manner, the barrel, forged solidly from a bar of cast steel, is bored and completed to calibre and is then submitted to the various operations of planning, grooving the lower projection, beneath the barrel, with which the base pin is ultimately connected, tapped, and then rifled by a self-adjusting machine, which gives to the longitudinal grooves, the form of a contracting pitch spiral, commencing nearly straight at the lower end and terminating at the muzzle in a curve of much smaller radius.

All the various parts of the lock are made by machinery, each having its relative initial point to work from, and on the correctness of which the perfection depends.

So with the stock and the mountings, the ramrod lever, etc., all are formed and worked by different sets of machines.

In fact, all the separate parts travel independently through the manufactory, arriving at last, in an almost complete condition, in the hands of the finishing workmen, by whom they are assembled, from promiscuous heaps, and formed into firearms, requiring only the polishing and fitting demanded for ornament.

A large number of machines is necessarily required for these operations; as it has been found advantageous to confine each one to its peculiar province, rather than to employ any more comprehensive machine, for several operations.

By this system the machines become almost automatons, performing certain labour under the guidance of women, or children, and thus the economy and precision of the manufacture are insured.

The improvements which time and experience have gradually introduced, have at length brought this firearm to its present state and have rendered it the reliable and efficient weapon for field service which it has proved to be, in the actions between the American and Mexican armies.

The official reports to Congress from the officers serving in that war, establish the reputation of the arm, and this is confirmed by Major-General Taylor, late President of the United States, who whilst commanding the American Army in Mexico, wrote in these terms to the Author:

"I have been much pleased with an examination which I have made of your new modelled repeating pistols and feel satisfied, that under all circumstances, they may be safely relied on;" and this opinion is universally concurred in by the officers of the United States' Army and Navy, who have had ample opportunity of proving their efficiency in active service. Among others, Major Thornton, the Inspector of Firearms for the United States Army, stated, that "After much firing and examination, the Board of Ordnance adopted Colonel Colt's pistol for the service, as the best weapon presented for their consideration. Experiments showed, that six rounds of the pistol could be loaded and fired in a minute, with much greater accuracy and penetration than he had ever thought necessary for a pistol. A horseman could use it with one hand and have the other free to manage his horse. The dragoons and mounted riflemen should all be armed with these weapons, as in the hands of men accustomed to wield them, he considered them most efficient arms both for attack or defence."*

---

* The "New Quarterly Review" for July 1852, contains the following apposite remarks:—"We must now advert to the 'repeating principle,' as applied to firearms in general, but more especially to pistols and carbines. It is to our transatlantic friends that we are indebted for the perfection of these weapons, for though, more than two centuries ago, various attempts were made to produce a series of successive discharges from one arm, without the necessity for re-loading, it is to Colonel Colt's perseverance, energy, and mechanical skill, that the merit is due of having successfully vanquished all the difficulties that presented themselves in their construction.

Colonel Chalmers, R.A., has kindly furnished the diagrams of practice at Woolwich (Plate 2), made in the absence of the Author; with pistols taken

"Innumerable were the objections he had to contend with at the outset. Military men sneered at the idea as preposterous. 'They would always be liable to get out of order'—'They would take too long to re-load'—'They would besides always be missing fire,' etc., etc. The Colonel did not, as many under the circumstances would have done, sit down and wage an idle paper war with his opponents. He did better—he set to work and demonstrated, that they none of them knew anything whatever of the subject on which they were all so confident. It was, however, natural that prejudice should be roused against an innovation of the kind—no invention of any value was ever yet otherwise received.

"As regards the liability of the revolving pistol to get out of order, this was satisfactorily disproved, by a severe trial instituted by order of the Board of Ordnance of the United States, who directed a holster pistol to be discharged twelve hundred, and a belt pistol fifteen hundred times, cleaning them but once a day: after which ordeal neither of the pistols appeared to be in the slightest degree injured.

"With respect to the cost of production, as almost every part is formed by machinery, hand labour being only required in the finishing department, Colonel Colt seems likely permanently to retain in his own hands the business which his ingenuity has created, for he will, of course, always be in a position to undersell any imitators that may appear. Greater security is also obtained from the same cause, for we find that, upon 'proof,' only one barrel and one cylinder burst out of 2,082 manufactured in the year 1850. The most perfect uniformity of detail is attained from the mechanism employed, for the several parts of each class of weapon are precisely similar, so that if any become damaged on service, a great number of available arms can be immediately compounded of those which have been partially injured.

"The ramrod attached to these pistols consists of a very clever but simple compound lever, which, forcing the ball effectually home, hermetically seals the chamber containing the powder, and by the application of a small quantity of wax to the nipple before capping, the pistol may be immersed for hours in water without the chance of a miss-fire.

"The movements of the revolving chamber and hammer are admirably provided for. The breech, containing six cylindrical cells for holding the powder and ball, moves one-sixth of a revolution at a time; it can therefore only be fired when the chamber and the barrel are in a direct line. The base of the cylindrical breech being cut externally into a circular ratchet of six teeth (the lever which moves the ratchet being attached to the hammer), as the hammer is raised in the act of cocking, the cylinder is made to revolve, and to revolve in one direction only. While the hammer is falling, the chamber is firmly held in its position by a lever fitted for the purpose; when the hammer is raised, the lever is removed and the chamber released.

"So long as the hammer remains at half-cock the chamber is free, and can be loaded at pleasure. The rapidity with which these arms can be loaded is one of their great recommendations, the powder being merely poured into each receptacle in succession, and the balls being then dropped in upon it, without any wadding and driven home by the ramrod, which of course is never required to enter the barrel.

"While carried in the pocket, or belt, there is no possibility of an accidental discharge of these pistols. Whenever it is required to clean the barrel and chamber, they can be taken to pieces in a moment, wiped out, oiled, and replaced.

"The hammer at full cock forms the sight by which aim is taken. The pistol is readily cocked by the thumb of the right hand, a plan in every way far superior to the arrangement whereby the hammer is raised by a pull on the trigger; this is in every respect most objectionable, the pull materially interfering with the correctness of aim, and the sear-spring having the duty of the main-spring to perform as well, is apt constantly to be getting out of order. Not so Colonel Colt's; as regards the purposes for which they are intended they may be pronounced in every respect perfect.*

"The gallant Colonel has applied the same principle to a carbine, which, from the facility it offers for loading, is admirably adapted for cavalry.

---

* Since this article was in type, we have been informed that Colonel Colt has just established here a manufactory for his revolvers. The building he has fitted up for the purpose is the one at Thames-Bank, near Vauxhall Bridge, lately in the occupation of the workmen engaged in making the mouldings, &c., for the New Palace at Westminster.

indiscriminately from the Great Exhibition. They extend from the 13th to the 21st of October 1851, and exhibit extraordinary force and precision of firing.

With a large revolving pistol, at a distance of 50 yeards, out of sixty shots, five shots traversed the bull's-eye of 6 inches diameter, and thirty-nine shots hit within a square of 2 feet. Fig. 1.

In another case, at 50 yards, out of fifty-four shots, forty-six shots were placed within 2 feet square, of which six were in the bull's-eye. Fig. 2.

In the next case, at a distance of 100 yards, out of sixty-four shots, thirty-seven balls hit the target, of which two traversed the bull's-eye, twenty-seven missing the target; indicating that the sights were arranged for a shorter distance. Fig. 3.

With the small revolving belt pistol, out of forty-eight shots, at a distance of 50 yards, twenty-five shots hit within 1 foot square, of which thirteen were in the bull's-eye. Fig. 4.

In another case out of eighteen shots, at a distance of 50 yards, five traversed the bull's-eye, and all were lodged within 2 feet square. Fig. 5.

Further experiments will be made with these fire-arms, after being adapted to the standard percussion cap of the service, which the Author is preparing at the suggestion of the Board of Ordnance, as the present state of border warfare at the Cape, in India, and in other parts of the British Colonies, demands the adoption of repeating arms, and they must necessarily be adapted to the ordinary ammunition of the service.

The paper is illustrated by a series of diagrams from which Plate 1 and 2 are compiled.

"'Modern fire-arms,' observes an able contemporary, 'as used for purposes of war, are just now in a transition state. Since the invention of the percussion lock, but little attention has been paid in this country to their improvement. The ill-concealed contempt with which purely scientific attempts are received, by those who make their only boast of being "practical men," is nowhere so prevalent as in England, and accordingly we find, that while we have remained stationary, the great continental military powers and the United States have not only availed themselves of each improvement as it appeared, but have stimulated invention by liberal patronage. The result of this obstinate adherence to an antiquated system has, fortunately, not yet been tested by an European war. Can we doubt what would be the result of an engagement between two bodies of troops, one armed with the English musket and the other with the needle-gun, which, taking the number of shots only into account, is 3½ times as effective? Or, in the case of a frigate engagement, what would be the fate of any boarding party having to face a body of men armed with Colt's "six-shooters?" What an eager rush would there be to wipe off the burning disgrace! What sums would be squandered in trying to do that in a few months, which had occupied other nations years! The "practical men," no doubt, would attempt to console us, by calculating how many needle-guns and revolvers had got out of order during the campaign, and how bravely English soldiers stood up to be shot at by an almost invisible enemy.'

"As might be imagined, Colonel Colt's invention has called forth a host of imitations. We have examined and carefully tested these successively, and with the exception of two, or three, found them to be all decidedly inferior to the American original, which, of course, being protected by patent, cannot be copied in its main essentials. Consequently, none of the English revolvers have either the lever ramrod, or the separation between the nipples, which Colonel Colt regards as most essential."

DESCRIPTION OF PLATES 1 AND 2.

Plate 1.

	Page
Fig. 1. A Matchlock Gun, in the Tower of London. (Supposed to be of the 15th Century)	4
" 2. Ditto, brought from India by Lord William Bentinck	5
" 3. A Pyrites Wheel-lock Musketoon, in the Tower	ib.
" 4. A Pistol of similar construction to Fig. 3; in the Rotunda a Woolwich	6
" 5. An elaborately finished Spanish un of the 18th Century; in the Rotunda at Woolwich	ib.
" 6. An Arm of similar construction to Fig. 5; in the Tower	7
" 7. A Gun obtained from Messrs. Forsyth and Co.; apparently not more than a century old	ib.
" 8. A rotating clambered breech Gun with Flint Lock; patented in 1818 by E. H. Collier, United States, America	9
" 9. Section of a Pistol, constructed by the Author at an early stage of the invention	11
" 10. Application of the principle to Rifles and Muskets	12
" 11. A Rifle made by the Author in 1836 to rotate and fire by the continued action of the lever, or by introducing a trigger	12
" 12, 13, 14. Carbine and Pistols, as now made at Colonel Colt's Manufactory, at Hartford, Connecticut, United States, America	16
" 15. A Skeleton Arm, to show the various parts	ib.
" 16. A combination of a Bowie-knife with a Repeating Pistol, whose chamber rotates and the firing is effected by the same action of the trigger; made by Colonel Colt in 1836	24

Plate 2.

Figs. 1 to 5. Diagrams of practice at Woolwich; with Pistols taken indiscriminately from the Great Exhibition in 1851	20

Colonel COLT, in answer to questions from the President, explained, that the course of this invention did not differ from that of almost every other innovation; it had to combat the prejudices of those using the old arms and the interested opposition of the manufacturers, and on that account he had been driven, not only to labour at attaining simplicity and efficiency in the arms themselves, but to contrive and adapt the tools and machinery for their production, with uniformity and rapidity and at the lowest cost. After he had undergone all the anxiety, labour and risk, attendant on bringing the arms to their present state, it was objected that the idea was not new, indeed that from an early period, repeating fire-arms with revolving chamber-breeches had been well known; he was now aware of this fact, but when he first commenced his experiments, he had not the most remote notion of anything of the kind having ever been previously attempted. At that time he was a very young man, and with only limited mechanical knowledge.

His first invention was a fire-arm which would, in these days, be considered a very clumsy affair, although it was very similar to several of the weapons now being made in this country, and which were asserted to be superior to his pistols. It was necessary to explain, that the weapons first made were almost skeleton arms, but when he took out his patent and commenced their manufacture, the front end of the revolving-chamber was closed in, and the base end covered with a shield, to make the arm look well; the consequence was, that simultaneous explosion of several chambers frequently occurred, and this serious defect was only remedied by removing the plate, and the shield, and chamfering the orifices of the chambers. The first weapons also were made to be cocked and fired by the same action of pulling the trigger, but it was found impossible to take a certain aim with them, as it was necessary to exert as much force with the finger, as would overcome the resistance of the main spring in cocking, and the weapon deviated from the line of sight; besides which it could not be carried on half cock and was liable to explode the cap, if it received any accidental concussion.

Fig. 16, Plate 1, a combination of a bowie-knife and repeating pistol, made in 1836, would explain what he meant and show how objectionable such an arrangement was in practice. Another modification consisted in having a ring trigger beneath the lock, on pulling which the hammer was raised and the chamber rotated, whilst the gun was fired by pulling an ordinary trigger. This construction required four, or five, additional parts in the lock. At last, the present simple arrangement was arrived at, and he believed that it was almost impossible to have an accident, from the simultaneous explosion of several caps, or chambers, or to injure the weapons without subjecting them to very rough usage, and the perfection of their fitting was so great that they had been fired after immersion in water or lying in the open air for a length of time.

The Honorable ABBOTT LAWRENCE, U.S. Minister, said no words of his could so emphatically, or thoroughly express the general approval of these arms, as the Report to Congress of the Committee on Military Affairs, printed January 30, 1851, wherein it was stated that experience had proved how difficult is was to contend successfully against savages with the usual arms of mounted men, the ordinary dragoon pistol and carbine; whilst General Harney, an experienced officer, who had successfully used Colt's arms in Florida stated that they were the only weapons with which the United States' troops could ever hope to subdue the wild and daring tribes, against whom they were called to act; but that with them, a few bold men, well skilled in the use of these weapons, could encounter and scatter almost any number of savages.

Being a civilian, Mr. Lawrence only knew the merits of these weapons from general reputation, and from their having been adopted by the United States' Government, after long trials and considerable experience in their use. In the army generally, they were considered the most efficient weapons ever introduced, particularly for border warfare, against savage tribes whose cunning hardihood, courage and skill, rendered them very formidable enemies. It was his opinion that the British troops would never successfully oppose the Kaffirs, until they were supplied with these repeating fire-arms, and he was much gratified that one of his countrymen should have produced a weapon, which was admitted, as far as it was yet known in Europe, to be superior to any other arm of the kind, and he was assured this gratification would be participated in by all around him, as they must remember that the British and the Americans were brethren, sprung from the same Anglo-Saxon stock, speaking the same language, and inheriting the same feelings which animated the subjects of these realms. He felt convinced, that the arm would have a fair trial in England, that no undue prejudice would be permitted to prevail, and that the invention would be examined and tested as if it had been brought forward by a British subject. There was room enough for inventions of all countries, and all that could be desired was, that in a fair and proper spirit of rivalry, this invention should be considered and examined with that good feeling and kindness which should animate all men, in the great cause of promoting the arts and sciences, and the application of science to art.

When he came to the meeting he had not any idea of being called on to express an opinion, but having risen, he must thank the members for the manner in which they had received his countryman's paper, and he trusted, that through apparently a warlike subject, its discussion would be as productive of harmony in the Institution, as the general use of the weapons in warfare would certainly be productive of peace, for the most effective weapons were the most efficient peace-makers, and though he was himself a peacable man, in every sense of the word, he was convinced that to maintain peace it was necessary always to be prepared for war; every improvement in fire-arms, therefore, reduced the cruelty of war, and tended to the perpetuation of peace, and hence he should be an advocate for any improvement, which would tend to diminish the ravages of war, whether between civilized nations, or against savage tribes, in the now inevitable spread of the white man, in his course of emigration.

Commodore Sir THOMAS HASTINGS, R.N., regretted that he could add but little interest to the discussion, as the paper had fully described the weapon and its merits; he must however state that Colonel Colt had afforded the officers of the Ordnance every facility, for attaining a complete knowledge of its merits, or defects, and he believed the general impression was that no fire-arm of that size ever possessed so much power. It must be acknowledged, that war was a great evil, particularly between civilized nations, but it was equally true, that giving the utmost perfection to the weapons used, was the surest manner of annihilating modern warfare. It was well known that in some of the great battles of the ancients more combatants fell, than during a whole campaign of modern armies, and in the battle of Lepanto, the last great hand-to-hand fight, fifty thousand combatants fell, which exceeded the numbers killed in all the naval engagements of the last and present centuries. Every step towards perfection, in weapons of war, was a humane improvement, and on that ground, independently of the necessity of arming the troops in the most efficient manner, the attention of the Ordnance had been carefully directed towards these and other improved arms, and the result of the trials had been to convince him and other officers, that they had rarely seen better practice, than with Colt's pistols. The ordinary infantry musket was considered a useful weapon at one hundred yards, but beyond that distance, it was mere random firing; now Colt's large pistol was equal in effect to the musket, at that range, and for use against savage tribes it must be a most effective weapon. The tactics of the Kaffirs were to tease an out-post sentry, at a distance, until they had drawn his fire, and then to spring on him before he had time to reload; and in attacking a convoy, which was generally done in a defile, a rush was made, which induced the fire of the whole guard and the men were left defenceless, except by the bayonet, which was not effective against long lances, or assagais. Now nothing could be more perfectly adapted to meet these tactics, than the revolvers, because after the savages had received the musket shots, they would rush up in a body to close quarters and thus render the effect of the pistols more certain. After a few experiments of this kind, the savages would have become acquainted with the nature of the weapon and the convoys might almost be sent without escort. He was of opinion that these arms would be found extremely useful for troops on special duty and eventually it might be advantageous to introduce them generally into both services.

Captain Sir E. BELCHER, R.N., said that some time ago he was in Texas, among the American troops, and there saw Colt's revolvers used with great effect and precision, and had never heard of an accident occurring from simultaneous explosion of the chambers. They were generally used by the mounted Rangers, who appeared to rely on them, for their effective attacks on the enemy.

He would suggest to Colonel Colt, whether it might not be advantageous so to modify the form, as to make the breech end of the barrel conical, and to introduce it into the mouth of the rotating chamber, in order to prevent the loss of power arising from the present escape of lateral fire, between the chamber and the barrel, and to throw the fire obliquely forward. In the old Chinese jinghals this arrangement was made, evidently from experience of its utility.

Colonel COLT explained that such an arrangement, as had been suggested by Sir E. Belcher, had been tried and was in fact now used, in some of the imitations of his revolvers, but it added to the complexity of the weapon, which he had desired to reduce to the utmost simplicity, and it was not found, in practice, that any serious loss of power resulted from the small escape of the lateral fire, that actually took place in his revolvers, as from the accurate fighting of the several parts, the mouth of the chamber was brought into very close proximity with the base of the barrel, and yet permitted the free rotation of the chamber.

Sir THOMAS HASTINGS agreed with Colonel Colt that there was not any necessity for the arrangement suggested by Sir E. Belcher; since everything which detracted from the simplicity of construction of the weapon, must be prejudicial to it, and the essential difference between the Chinese jinghal and Colt's revolver was, that the former was a cumbrous, unwieldy instrument, whereas in the latter there was, in the least possible compass, a weapon which, in the hands of men conversant with its use, would do as good service as the ordinary musket and could throw five, or six balls without stopping to reload. The reports of trials made under the superintendence of the Officers of the Board of Ordnance, clearly pointed out these advantages, and those gentlemen acted so conscientiously and made their reports with such fidelity, that perfect reliance could be placed in all their statements. He made these observations because he saw on the walls some diagrams of the firing at targets, at Woolwich, which corroborated his opinion of the utility of these arms; and it was only justice to Colonel Colt to do so, as since his arrival in England, that gentleman had afforded every facility for the perfect understanding of the arm of which he was the inventor.

Sir T. Hastings entirely participated in the feelings so ably expressed by the Hon. Mr. Lawrence, and trusted that the relations with our Transatlantic brethren, and indeed with all the civilized world, would long remain on a footing of the strictest amity.

Captain RIDDELL, R.A., said that such ample opportunities for proving the utility of the revolvers had been afforded, and such a clear account of the invention had been given in this paper, that it was incumbent on him, as a British officer, to add his thanks to Colonel Colt, for the efficient arm he had introduced to the notice of the Government and which, he did not doubt, would soon be employed for those branches of the service in which it was so well calculated to be useful.

Mr. A. B. RICHARDS said that through the courtesy of Colonel Colt, with whom he had no previous acquaintance, he had ample opportunity of trying the revolvers, and having some considerable experience in the use of fire-arms, he ventured to state, that he never had met with any pistol which carried with greater precision. Out of six shots from one cylinder, five of the balls touched each other in the target, at a distance of fifteen paces, in a shooting gallery. He did not think that greater accuracy could be required, nor could it generally be attained without hair-triggers. For active service, particularly against the Kaffirs, this weapon would evidently be invaluable, and he felt convinced that the authorities would soon see the propriety of adopting it.

Major-General Sir C. PASLEY, R.E., had not officially any experience of the weapons under discussion, but he had examined them attentively and knowing the care with which the trials for the Board of Ordnance were conducted, and seeing the results, he formed a high opinion of their merits, particularly as subsidiary arms for troops engaged in warfare against savage tribes, or on special and detached service, and he felt assured these capabilities would be fully appreciated by the proper authorities.

Mr. J. FREEMAN said that during the course of the Great Exhibition, he had been attracted, in the American department, to Colonel Colt's revolvers, and perceived their merits; he begged however to direct attention to a pistol on a somewhat similar principle, made by Messrs. Deane, Adams, and Deane, and would ask one of those gentlemen to explain wherein its merits consisted.

Fig. 2.

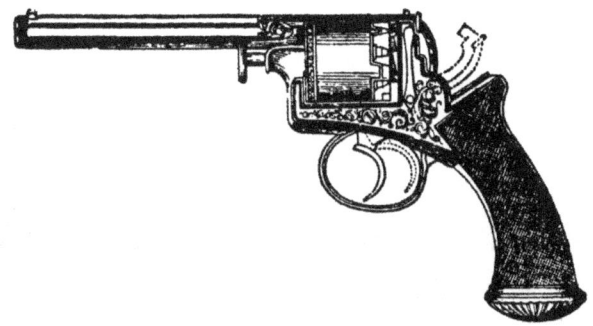

Mr. ADAMS, exhibited and described a revolver of his invention. (Woodcut Fig. 2.) The barrel, the lock-frame and top-bar were all forged out of one piece of iron; the chamber to contain five charges, revolved on a centre pin, which could be either drawn entirely, or partially out, as was required and was held in its position by a side spring; the toothed ratchet was secured to the base of the chamber by two screws, so as to admit of its being renewed, when it was abraded by use, and motion was given to it by a ratchet pall, connected with the hammer, which was lifted by pulling the trigger. The hammer moved on a transverse pin, and was pressed down on the nipple, by a back spring in the stock, being connected with it by a swivel link; the trigger was kept in position by a horizontal bent spring, and had attached to it the hammer-lifter and the ratchet pall; the point of the former fell into a notch in the base of the hammer, so that as the trigger was pulled, the hammer was raised, until the rounded portion of the base, acting as a cam, forced the lifter out of the notch, and allowed the hammer to descend on the nipple and to explode the percussion-cap. On withdrawing the finger from the trigger, the lifter and ratchet pall descended and again slipped into the notches of the hammer and the chamber, in readiness for repeating the operation of firing. The lifter was retained in contact with the hammer, by a small flat spring, the upper end of which was attached to the pall, while the lower end acted upon the lifter, which, in turning on its centre, brought the lower prologation against the spring, below the centre, so as to press the upper end in the proper direction, in order that its action might be certain.

The rotation of the chambers was obtained by a ratchet pall, acting on a tooth each time the trigger was pulled, thus causing the chambers to revolve, so far as to bring a nipple into the proper position for receiving the blow of the hammer, and in that situation it was held by a projecting stop on the back of the trigger.

In order to load the chambers, it was necessary that they should revolve free of the stop; this was effected by pressing inwards another stop, attached to a spring on the side of the lock, which engaged the point of the hammer and prevented it from descending on the nipple, until the chambers were loaded, when on the trigger being pulled, the side spring stop was released and resumed its original position, leaving the weapon ready for action.

The bullets were cast with a small "tang" on them, which served to fix a wad on each, thus no ramrod was required in loading, the bullets being merely pressed in with the finger. The aperture of the barrel was slightly expanded at the lower end, to admit of the bullets entering more readily in firing. The rifling of the barrel was the reverse of the ordinary system, as it consisted of three projecting "feathers," or ridges, extending the length of the tube, leaving very wide grooves between them.

It would be observed, that the cocking and firing were performed by the same action of the trigger; therefore the rapidity of firing was proportionally great; the arm was very light, its construction simple, and its action certain.

With respect to the mode of manufacture, every portion to which self-acting tools had been found applicable, was planned, bored, turned, slotted and rifled by machinery.

Mr. A. B. RICHARDS inquired, whether the principle of the weapon just described by Mr. Adams, was not indentical with that brought before the public many years ago, in connection with a pistol with five, or six, revolving barrels, which he believed had been laid aside, because it was found, that after being used for a short time, the spring did not detain sufficient power to bring down the hammer with force enough to explode the cap, and if the spring was made stronger, it required the exertion of so much strength, that the weapon was depressed in firing, and taking a correct aim was nearly impossible. There did not appear to be any advantage in the power of firing so rapidly, as on service it was certainly not necessary to put five, or six, bullets into the same adversary, and whilst directing Colt's revolvers from one point to another, there was no difficulty in cocking the pistol with the thumb, using only one hand.

He begged also to ask, whether a paper, headed "Experiments with Fire-arms," dated "Woolwich, 10th September 1851," purporting to be a report of some trials of Colonel Colt's and Mr. Adams' revolvers, was issued officially, as the results were very different from those which were generally understood to have been attained; and as the paper appeared to have been extensively circulated, it was well to arrive at a true understanding of its value.

Sir T. HASTINGS stated that so far as he was cognizant of the matter, no report of the comparative merits of Colonel Colt's and Mr. Adams' revolvers had been officially published by the Board of Ordnance.

Captain RIDDELL corroborated the statement of Sir T. Hastings.

The SECRETARY, at the request of the President, read two communications from Colonel Chalmers, R.A., relative to the diagrams of practice with Colonel Colt's arms,* permitted by him to be transmitted to the Institution, in which he stated "I have seen the printed document entitled 'Experiments with Fire-arms,' as published by Mr. Adams; it is not official."—"I have

---

* Vide ante p. 20, and Plate 2.

for some time had two of Colonel Colt's revolvers under severe trial, and with good caps they never miss fire."

Mr. PLINY MILES said the principle of construction of Mr. Adams' revolver had been tried in America long ago, and had been abandoned. Colonel Colt had at one time fallen into the error of using it, as was evident from the bowie-knife pistol exhibited. Mr. Miles carried a weapon like that described by Mr. Adams, for nearly two years, in the Western States and the valley of the Mississippi, but he never could make it a serviceable arm, as it required the exertion of so much strength in the finger, to revolve the cylinder, and lift the hammer by the same pull on the trigger, as fired the charge, that the muzzle was almost invariably depressed, or turned out of range, and he never could be certain of hitting a mark: he therefore got rid of it, and purchased one of Colt's revolvers, which he found just as effective as the other was inefficient. He now rarely missed a shot, even at birds, and the revolving of the cylinder, being performed by the operation of cocking, the firing could be rendered almost as delicate as by a hair-trigger, so that the most accurate aim could be taken.

Mr. C. MAY, as the only member of the Society of Friends present, rose to order: he thought the meeting had erred, in quitting the question of the mode of manufacture of these weapons, for a discussion upon their relative merits, or their destructive qualities, which he submitted, were not proper topics for the Institution of Civil Engineers; he thought all weapons might be dispensed with, except for protection against wild beasts.

From an examination of the specimens before the meeting, he was of opinion, that the machinery used in the manufacture was not of the accurate description generally employed in this country, the tool marks were more evident, than in the machine-made work produced at Manchester, and no information had yet been given as to the price of production. He begged Colonel Colt to give such information on these points as he considered could with propriety be imparted to the meeting.

Mr. RENDEL, V.P., agreed with Mr. May, that the efficiency of the arms was a question which would be more properly considered by the authorities at Woolwich; it would be more interesting to the meeting to know what kind of machinery was used in the manufacture of the arms, and to be informed what process each piece went through, in arriving at the state to form component parts of so apparently well-constructed a weapon, as that now submitted by Colonel Colt, who he would beg to enter into such details as he judged fit, relative to the manufacture.

Colonel COLT said, he thought the process of manufacturing had been fully described in the paper, as could be done without prolixity; he would however revert to whatever had been omitted in the paper, or in the previous part of the discussion; but it was scarcely practicable to give a clear idea of the process of manufacture, without diagrams of the machines employed, and even they would hardly convey a correct impression of the action of such tools.

Each separate piece of the arm, was forged hot, under swages, and then underwent a series of operations in machines, each adapted especially for one peculiar service. This had been found more economical than using comprehensive tools, and a greater degree of uniformity of structure was obtained. The mode of proceeding with one part would give an idea of that for all the rest. Taking, for instance, the lock frame; the swaged block of metal was held in clamps, and the centre hole drilled and tapped for the base pin, which was then inserted, in order that each subsequent operation should have relation to, and accord with the position of that part of the arm, which served as a common centre. The lower inside curve was then cut, the various slots, grooves, spring bearings, &c., were cut through clamps, by which the piece was presented to the various automaton machines, and last of all, the operations of centring, drilling and tapping all the holes were performed, also under the guidance clamps. That piece passed through twenty-two distinct operations, and after leaving the last machine, it was only requisite to remove by hand the rough edges left by the tools; thus a clear idea could be formed of the amount of manual labour employed.

In making the cylinder, or chamber, which was also forged from a block of steel, annealed, the centre hole was first drilled, then the exterior was turned and engraved (also by a machine), then the ratchet teeth were cut out of the solid metal, because it had been found, that the ratchets, which were attached by screws, were apt to get loosened by service and the arms were rendered inefficient and dangerous; the holes for the nipples, and the charge chambers were then bored on a kind of universal chuck, the muzzles were chamfered, the stop grooves cut and the cylinder was completed fit for use.

The barrel forged solid, by swages, from a bar of steel, was first bored, and then rifled by a very simple machine, in such a manner as that the groove, at the breech end, was almost straight, and gradually contracted the pitch to a sharp curve at the muzzle, to give to the bullet the proper rotation in delivery; the exterior of the barrel was then finished in the various machines and the lever ramrod was attached.

It was unnecessary to extend this kind of description of processes, which would be readily understood by all engineers, and it must be evident, that a degree of uniformity and precision was arrived at, which could not be attained by any other means. Nor could the quantity required be produced by manual labour; in his factory at Hartford, there were now thirty thousand weapons in various stages of progress, and the demand was so great, that he contemplated increasing the number of fifty-five thousand, to meet the requirement of the market; three hundred persons were employed, and about one hundred arms were finished per diem.[*] This must be evident proof of the paramount necessity for machinery, wherever combination might interfere with the work being done, and more especially in a country like the United States, where manual labour really could not have been procured, to produce such a quantity, independently of the great merit of the positive uniformity of the arms, which had been proved, by picking

---

[*] It has since been stated, that by further subdivision of the operations, and by additional machinery, two hundred and fifty pistols have been finished per diem, or fifteen hundred arms per week have been completed at the Hartford factory, by less than five hundred workpeople.—*Sec. Inst. C. E.*

up the disabled arms after an action, when seventy-five per cent, of perfect weapons were readily made up fit for use.

In round numbers it might be stated, that supposing the cost of an arm to be 100, of this the wages of those who attended to, and passed the pieces through the machines was 10 per cent, and those of the best class of workmen engaged in putting together, finishing and ornamenting the weapons, was also 10 per cent; thus leaving 80 per cent for the duty done by the machinery.

The weights of the several weapons were—

	lbs.	oz.
The Army, or Holster Pistol	4	4
The Navy, or Belt Pistol	2	6
The Pocket Pistol, 6-inch Barrel	1	12
Ditto 5-inch Barrel	1	10
Ditto 4-inch Barrel	1	8
Ditto 3-inch Barrel	1	6

Mr. HODGE was happy to have an opportunity of adding his testimony to the merits of Colonel Colt's weapons, and to the simplicity and effectiveness of the machinery employed in their manufacture. The skill displayed in the design of the various machines, was very remarkable, but it was evidently the result of necessity, arising from the difficulty and expense of obtaining skilled labour in the United States; this had stimulated the inventive faculties of all engaged in the mechanical pursuits and as a general rule, nothing was made by hand that could be executed by machinery. Perhaps one of the most striking evidences of practical skill was the variety of crooked cutters used for shaping, not only in Colonel Colt's armoury, but in all the machinery factories in America, and it would answer the purpose of English manufacturers, to send an intelligent foreman over to the States, to examine what was now being done there. The gunmakers at Birmingham might certainly learn much from studying Colonel Colt's system of manufacturing, and their work would be produced at infinitely less cost, if they abandoned the system of employing a number of men, each working independently in his own ill-lighted, badly ventilated, and inconvenient workshop, forming and filing up, without any uniformity, parts of arms, which would be produced in much larger quantities, in less time and with perfect identity of form, by the simple machines used by the Americans.

He thought much was due to the greater amount of intelligence to be found among the working classes in the States, than among the corresponding class in England. Most of the American mechanics were not only good handy-craftsmen, but from their habits of thought and determination to "go a-head," were continually devising means of executing their work with rapidity; thus new machines were constantly invented, and the education and intelligence of the working classes increased daily, because there was stimulus for thought and a consciousness in the mind of every man, that there was an ample field before him, in which he must prosper, if he used any exertion. It was ardently to be hoped, that by the extension of education among the working mechanics in England, the intelligence and inventive genius, which at present appeared confined in a great measure to a certain class, would extend to the working mechanics, whose manual skill was beyond all praise.

Colonel COLT, in answer to questions by Professor Cowper, explained, that the majority of the tools used were revolving cutters, at a slow speed for heavy coarse work, and with great velocity for fine finishing, or light operation; in slotting, shaping, and drilling, the tools were guided by steel clamps, which insured that uniformity in the several parts, which was one of the distinguishing features of his manufacture. Special machines were used, for all special operations, as general planing machines had not been found advantageous.

Mr. HODGE said that although revolving cutters were certainly used in machine shops in England, they were not employed to the extent they might be; it was, however, the use of the shaping cutter that should be more extensively introduced; he had never seen such good work in any factory as in Colonel Colt's, and it must be entirely attributed to the judicious use of the tools he had mentioned.

The machine for rifling two barrels at the same time, by means of an excentric wheel, was very beautiful, and he must repeat his regret that machines were not more used in the manufacture of arms in this country.

Mr. EVANS stated that in the year 1822 he manufactured a number of flint lock revolving chambered-breech firearms, for Mr. E. H. Collier, whose patent, with that of Mr. Coolidge, had been mentioned in the paper.* Those arms were chiefly made by machinery which was still in his possession.

Mr. Evans had also made machinery for the Government establishment at Enfield, by order of Mr. Lovell, Inspector General of Small Arms, and the arms made there were, to a considerable extent, produced by those machines.† The rifling especially was so executed, and the machine permitted the pitch of the groove to be varied, according to the will of the operator.

MR. HODGE expressed his gratification at hearing from Mr. Evans, that machinery had been introduced into the Government Small Arms Manufactory, as Mr. Hodge had suggested it to Mr. Evans six years ago and had for some time pressed it unavailingly on his notice.

MR. C. MAY begged to inquire of those who were well acquainted with the working classes in both countries, whether it was their deliberate opinion, that the American mechanics were better educated than their brethren in England. He had not been in the States, but from all he could collect he had arrived at the conviction that the best English mechanics were better than the Americans; and he must say that no work he had ever seen from America was equal to that produced in the machine shops of Manchester, Leeds, and other places, enjoying a reputation for good work.

* Vide ante page 9.   † Vide ante page 17.

MR. GLYNN was much inclined to agree with Mr. May, and the eminence so frequently, and at times so rapidly, attained by English mechanics, would seem to corroborate those views: indeed there was scarcely any field in which more men had risen to distinction, by the exercise of skill and talent, than in civil and mechanical engineering. This could not be the case, if they had not education as well as innate talent.

MR. HAWKSHAW was of opinion, that if the term "education," meant "book-learning," the working classes in America, particularly in the cotton factories, possessed a greater amount of education, than the corresponding class in England; but if "education" meant the special instruction, which enabled a working mechanic to perform his daily labour, with credit to himself and with profit to his employer, the English mechanics were the better educated class. He, however, thought that as far as general education was concerned, the American workmen might be considered as more advanced.

MR. J. SCOTT RUSSELL apprehended, that the comparison must be drawn between the better men of the working classes and not between the mere handicraftsmen, who he believed to be nearly identical in attainments in both countries. He thought that Mr. May must have formed his opinion from observations made at that paradise for the workmen, the works of Messrs. Ransomes and May, at Ipswich, where they were generally better educated, better conducted and better cared for, by their employers, than in almost any other establishment he had ever visited. Now Mr. Russell did entertain some alarm as to the ultimate position of English mechanics, with respect to that of the workmen in Prussia and in other parts of the continent. For the last fifteen years, the artisans of Germany had been receiving an amount of education, which could not fail, eventually, to render them formidable competitors, unless the English workman added education to his present, almost matchless, manipulative skill. He was glad, that the subject of the education of the working classes had been mentioned at the Institution, because he felt assured, it was from thence, that the first movement should emanate, for the introduction of a comprehensive scheme of education for that valuable class of men, the English mechanics.

MR. W. B. ADAMS said the men worked harder in the United States, under the influence of better wages, but he did not think the produce was generally so well finished as in England. There was certainly room for a greater extent of education among the working mechanics here, and more especially for instruction in the mechanical principles of the tools and machines, the application of which was their daily occupation. The employers would find great benefit result, from encouraging and even enforcing education among the working classes.

MR. HEPPEL said he had for some time a considerable number of Prussian workmen in his employment, manufacturing engines and general machinery; they were better informed on general topics, but the English mechanics made themselves more really valuable, by their more positive knowledge of their duties, their greater appreciation of the necessity of precision and of accurate adjustment, and their greater readiness in emergencies.

The Hon. ROBERT JAMES WALKER (late Secretary U. S. Treasury) said he rose with diffidence to speak of civil engineering, in an assembly where the best authorities were continually heard on that important subject; his attention had been chiefly directed to finance, political economy, and jurisprudence, but he was fully alive to the advantages of cultivating a science which conferred such inestimable benefits on mankind generally. He felt but little qualified to enlarge on the character and use of the celebrated revolver, of his friend and countryman Colonel Colt, as the principal object of his social and political course had been, to encourage free commerce and intercourse between all countries and thus to render gunpowder and fire-arms unknown quantities in the future career of England and America.

It must be evident to all thinking men, that civil engineering was one of the most important professions connected with the advance and progress of the human race. To that profession was due the praise of having constructed railroads, bridges, and canals—improving rivers and harbours—building steam engines, for locomotion upon land and water—and substituting machinery for manual labour, (greatly for its benefit) in nearly all industrial pursuits.

To the engineers must be attributed the construction, in the United States, of nearly 4,000 miles of canals, and upwards of 10,000 miles of railroads; and by their aid, at least one great railroad would be constructed across the American continent, from the Atlantic to the Pacific.

By the aid of the same great profession, a ship canal would no doubt, eventually, be cut through the American isthmus. This would be, in its consequences, the greatest work of civil engineering yet undertaken by man; and the American pioneers, now engaged in the preliminary railroad, would be greatly pleased, to obtain the aid of the Institution of Civil Engineers, and of its distinguished members, in connection with their own eminent engineers, in promoting the speedy construction of that great work, not only for the benefit of England and America, but of the world at large.

Civil engineering was the application of mind to matter, and was perhaps more important in its general effects, in America, than in Europe, inasmuch as labour being much dearer in America than in England, it became necessary, in order to enter into successful competition, to substitute more machinery for manual labour, in all manufacturing operations, and thus the inventive faculties were roused, and innumerable machines were introduced which, but for necessity, would never have been thought of. And here he might be permitted to remark, that, whilst it would not perhaps be possible at present to assemble in America so large a number of distinguished and scientific engineers, as were found in this Institution, yet he thought that education was more widely diffused among the industrial classes in the United States; that among the operatives, there were more educated heads at work than in England; and that must in a great degree be received as one of the chief causes of the progress and success of America. The educated industrial classes applied their intellect, from day to day, to improvements in the operations in which they are concerned, and hence it was, that many of the most useful inventions and discoveries had originated with the working mechanic handicraftsman.

With respect to the repeating fire-arms, the account of which had been read to the meeting, he was bound to state that during the last war with Mexico, the use of those weapons became a subject of careful discussion in the American Cabinet, of which he was then a member. From the evidence laid before the members, the decision was unanimously in favour of the employment of Colonel Colt's revolvers, in conformity with the recommendations of the distinguished officers who had used them. The results were most brilliant and successful in those campaigns, more especially in guerilla warfare; and he believed, that the sentiment of the army, the navy, and those who were from necessity obliged to be prepared for offensive, or defensive warfare, was clearly and decidedly in favour of the general use of Colt's repeating fire-arms.

General MacNeill hoped he might be permitted to revert very briefly to the merits of the repeating arms invented by his friend and countryman Colonel Sam Colt; he used the term "invented" advisedly, because he was aware of the progressive steps, by which the present efficient form of the weapon had been arrived at; he knew also, that Colonel Colt was not cognizant of any previous attempts to produce such weapons, until he visited Europe to secure his first patents, and he had watched, with more than ordinary interest, the gradual application of the ingenious self-acting tools employed in the manufacture of those arms.

As an old military man he had the means of obtaining the private opinions of most of the distinguished officers of all grades, whose public testimony of the merits of the arms in actual warfare, was embodied in the "Report of the Committee on Military Affairs" addressed to the Senate of the United States, January 30th, 1851 (31st Congress, 2nd Session) and without trespassing on the time of the meeting by entering into particulars, which had been so extensively circulated in that report, he might state, that all military men coincided in the opinion, that for detached service, reconnoitering parties, convoys, out-post sentries, and generally for service against savage tribes, or border warfare, Colt's repeating arms were most efficient and it was an acknowledged fact, that without their use, the late campaigns of the United States armies could not have been so speedily, or so satisfactorily terminated. It was proverbially difficult to induce old soldiers to try new weapons, and there had been the usual amount of reluctance to try, and then to recommend the adoption of the repeating arms, but there was no resisting the evidence of actual practice, and the demand for them in the frontier corps, soon became as urgent, as it was among the borders, who were not so slow to appreciate the advantages of such weapons.

The machinery used in the manufacture of these arms was equally remarkable for its simplicity, the ingenuity displayed in the adaptation of the tools, and the satisfactory manner in which all the various processes were conducted, so as to produce weapons, that were not only trustworthy and efficient, but so perfectly identical in all their parts, that in assembling a pistol, the several pieces were taken promiscuously from a heap, and the arm was finished almost without manual labour. It must be evident, that this was a great advantage, in a country where labour was so costly and where the borders, the isolated pioneers of civilization, who most required these weapons, must repair them, as well as use them.

As however it had been General MacNeill's lot, for many years past, to devote his energies to the peaceful occupations of Civil Engineering, he would prefer reverting to the subjects so well alluded to by the Hon. Mr. Walker, and he trusted, that in future the only contest between England and America, would be for priority in undertaking, and rapidity in executing, great engineering works for the benefit of the human race. In no ways could this desirable end be so well attained, as by combining the energy and comprehensive enterprise of American engineers, with the proverbial science, skill, intelligence and good faith of the English engineers, who would find in the United States a hearty welcome, and a fine field for the exercise of their professional talents.

It had been his good fortune, whilst actively engaged in the execution of extensive engineering works, to have under him many young men, Scotch, Irish, and English who all arrived with the same simple story, "they wanted work;" and though he could not give them such employment as their talents and acquirements warranted, he afforded them such occupation as he could command, and in a short time, though they might have commenced as mere chain draggers, or assistant surveyors, at the rate of a dollar per diem, they soon progressed, and in a few years some of them were realising large incomes. He did not claim any merit for thus advancing the career of these young men; they had served him well and obtained the just reward of their talents and integrity, but in all cases he felt that he was only returning, in a slight degree, the hospitality and kindness he had experienced, at the hands of Telford, George Stephenson, Walker, and other eminent engineers, when he visited England many years ago, as a young Captain of Engineers, with his brother officers Whistler and Knight, with whom he was associated, in a journey undertaken by order of the United States Government, for the inspection of the great works of art in Great Britain. On that occasion, it was his good fortune to be brought into contact with Mr. Robert Stephenson and Mr. Locke, at that time commencing the works which would hand down their names to posterity, as the worthy successors of the eminent men he had previously mentioned. He was proud to have known those two engineers, and to acknowledge, that whatever useful work he had undertaken, and whatever success he might have obtained in his own country, had been materially aided by the intercourse he had been permitted to have with those gentlemen at an early period of their professional career.

Since the period to which he alluded, a great change had taken place, in the means of acquiring engineering knowledge; at that time he was told, that "engineers, whose opinions were worth having, were too busy to write books;" but now at the meetings of the Institution, not only were papers brought forward and publicly discussed, but the most eminent authorities of all professions entered with interest into the debate, and the results were freely published to the world. Although perhaps there might not be the same class of works executed in the States, as in Great Britain, yet there was much originality in many of the works of American engineers, and it should be his study to induce a liberal interchange of scientific and professional communications, between the American societies and the Institution of Civil Engineers, and he was sure, that the Hon. Mr. Walker would induce the Government to transmit all the scientific documents published by its orders.

Science knew no distinction of country; the whole world was an open field for the exercise of engineering skill, and in that field, professional brethren of all nations should strive in the contest for the noble end of doing the greatest amount of good to the greatest number of the human race.

CHAPTER THREE

EXTRACTS FROM TESTIMONY GIVEN BY SAMUEL COLT IN LONDON, ENGLAND BEFORE A PARLIAMENTARY COMMITTEE

MARCH 1854

Lieutenant-Colonel Sam Colt, State of Connecticut, U. S. A. called in.

1085. "Do you consider that you make your pistols better by machinery than you could by hand labor?"

... "Most certainly."

1086. "And cheaper, also?"—"Much cheaper."

1087. "Are you familiar with the manufacture of muskets by machinery in America?"—"I am."

1088. "Do you consider that the muskets manufactured by machinery in America are as well fabricated as the Minie rifle which has been submitted to you?"—"There is none so badly made at our national armories as the Minie rifle shown to me; that arm would not pass one of our inspectors."

1089. "Do you consider that the muskets fabricated by machinery in America are much superior to the Minie rifle shown to you?"—"Most certainly I do."

1090. "Have you written to the Ordnance to consent, on certain terms, to supply muskets to the Ordnance?"—"I have written to the Ordnance my opinion of what the arms could be made for in England, but not with a view of taking a contract from that department, but to give my impression of what the arms could be made for in this country. I have indorsed that opinion by the statement that I would supply the arms at those prices."

1091. "Have you a copy of that letter?"—"Yes; this is the letter which I wrote to them" (handing in the same).

1092. "I will read this extract from your letter of the 13th of March. 'So confident am I that this system of manufacturing fire-arms is correct, and the only one by which arms can be made the one like the other, with economy, that I am free to say, what I have before verbally stated, that with one hundred thousand pounds expended in machinery, tools, &c., one million of rifled muskets can be produced at an expense of thirty shillings each; and that, while they will possess the advantage of uniformity of parts, none that are so made will be inferior to the best that can now be found in her Majesty's service for military purposes. I do not want to make a proposition of a contract for the construction of a million of arms that are not of my own peculiar principle, while you have men of ability, who, I believe, are fully competent to produce the one million of arms, if you desire me to do so, at the prices above named thirty shillings; and I would endeavor to do all the work in this country, unless I should be interrupted by conbinations of operatives claiming from me more than the present price of manual labor.' "—"That is all that could be said if I were to talk for a week; that is based on my estimates of what can be done; but if I had to do the work under restrictions that I do not now suffer, it could not be done, or it might not, because people might call upon me for extra service, extra pay, or extra something. If you can insure me the price of labor that I now pay, that result can be produced for that amount of money, with such and amount of outlay."

1102. Lord Seymour. "When did you first commence manufacturing small arms by machinery in America?"—"I commenced many years ago; I commenced in 1836, I think, first to make arms by machinery."

1103. "Since 1836, have you made any great improvements in the machinery?"—"Yes; I have made a great many improvements in the machinery, and every day adds an improvement now."

1104. "When you commenced at first to make arms, was it for the purpose of making arms for the Government of America, or for general sale?"—"For both. At first I intended it for private purposes, but with the hope of supplying Government, as all new mechanics think that Government patronage is valuable to them; it is an advertisement, if nothing else."

1105. "Would the same machinery that answered for the guns made for private purposes, answer also for the musket required for the Government of America?"—"Certainly it would."

1106. "The same machines will make, to a great extent, rifles, or fowling-pieces, or pistols?"—"To a certain extent. Most machinery is competent to many changes, so as to be made applicable to a pistol, to a rifle, to a musket, to a carbine, and to any other arm that you choose to apply it to. You only multiply the simpler engines where you have much to do, otherwise one universal machine would do all that you have to do. If I had one hundred arms to make a year, I should want only three or four machines; but if I had many hundred thousand arms to make, I must have many hundred machines, and then I would make each machine more stubborn and firm to do this particular work, and in proportion as it related to the quantity to be made."

1112. "You stated that you could make at the rate of one hundred thousand muskets a year; but you added, if no restrictions were put upon you?"—"No more than I have now."

1113. "Do you mean that the arms when made are not to be subject to any view?"—"I mean this: give me ten arms, the best you can pick out, to be models; pick me ten of the best Minie rifles (do not have them made on purpose): then pick out the best one, and I will more nearly resemble the best one with my one hundred thousand a year than the other nine will resemble one another."

1114. "You have stated that the best is very bad, and you have offered to make the arm of the Ordnance, but you say that the arm of the Ordnance is so badly made that it would not pass view in America?"—"Yes; our American inspectors are more strict than what I have yet seen in England; the arms must be more uniform. I do not say that we can make a single arm so well, or any better, but I say unqualifiedly this: give me one hundred arms to an American inspector, made at any place you choose by contract in England, and more would be condemned out of them, even if made expressly, than if you took the arms made by machiner, which shall be uniform in construction; you give to a man a model, and he will make them all alike; I can make a bad arm, and make bad arms all alike."

1115. "Are the Committee to understand that the fault which you find with the Ordnance is, that one arm is not like the other?"—"That is the very thing I find fault with in the arms I have seen here; there is more difference between one and another where they are made by hand, than there can possibly be when they are made by machinery. A machine tells better for uniformity than hand labor does; the eye cannot control the hand sufficiently to imitate a machine; it is the uniformity of the work that is wanted. If you give a model, even though a bad one, and if you instruct your operatives to attend the machine to make them like the model, they are all made bad; but if the model is right, the operative cannot change his machine, or get it out of place, and that is the effect of machinery on arms, or any other branch of mechanical industry."

1177. "As you consider the Ordnance arms to be badly made, do you think the barrel badly made?"—"I say it is simply bad for uniformity's sake. I say that you do not make any arms to interchange."

1118. "The fault you find with the arm is, in short, a want of uniformity of construction?"—"Yes."

1121. "Do you know, practically, whether in the arms made in America there has been this interchange?"—"Yes, many thousands; it is the constant habit of Government officers who use my arms in Oregon, or in California, to order one hundred mainsprings, or one thousand mainsprings, or one thousand hammers, or one thousand triggers, or one thousand of any thing else applicable to the most perishable parts of the arm, and I send them; and one of the commonest operatives or soldiers will take an ordinary tool, and put them in the place to which they belong. If the hammer is broken, he will put in a new one, and so on. Usually it is the custom in our country, where we send out a large number of arms, suppose one thousand, to California or Oregon, for military purposes, to put those parts to which accidents are most likely to occur in the arm-chests. A spring cannot always be relied on so much as a barrel, and we put enough in for immediate repair; and if there is a bad piece of metal thrown in, we supply it. Every thing goes under a particular form of gauge and proof, and an arm is repairable just as well in California as in New York. These remarks are applicable to the national musket, as well as to my own individual arms."

1124. "Their adoption of the manufacture of arms did not arise from the adaptation of machinery to that purpose, but it was before this new machinery was introduced?"—"They began by getting the best tools they could to start with, and continually improving upon them; for instance, improvements in stocking arouse from a man who had nothing in the world to do but to attend a common engine-turning lathe; he was turning gun-barrels, and as he came across that part of the barrel projecting for the pan, there was a part that he could not then turn by machinery. Mr. Blanchard said that he could, and being encouraged, did get an undulating motion in his lathe, and turn that part. That introduced a piece of machinery, and its principle ran through the whole of the Springfield Armory, till they finally produced not only that part better, but they went on till they produced an entire gun-stock by machinery. Now it costs less for a stock than it does here for the wood. At that armory this gun-stocking machinery has run on beyond any other branch in every department. That illustrates how far you can go; a man with any quantity of money can do any thing by machinery."

1137. "Am I right in concluding, that though the Government of America manufacture themselves a large amount of muskets, they yet find it good economy also to purchase of private manufacturers?"—"It may be more policy than economy."

1138. "Will you explain what you mean by 'more policy than economy?' —is it good policy to maintain the manufacture in the country?"—"Yes it is good policy to maintain a model shop in the country, if nothing more."

1139. "And it is worth while even for the Government of America to make some sacrifice in point of cheapness, in order to keep up the manufacture in the country?"—"I think it is good policy of any person who has to negotiate with another, always to hold within himself the power to produce that which he requires of another, and it is the same in the case of the Government of America as in the private transactions of life; they can produce at the national armories double what they now do; they do not do so; they wish to encourage the artisans of the country, and are willing to employ them. Suppose Government makes half, and contractors the other half, the result is the same; there is the same inspection; but for the Government to take the arms harem-scarem, they would not get the arms they wish for. Individuals sometimes, if there is more industry employed, and more economy employed in labor, may be able to make a little more profit out of it than the Government does, but that is the only way; it depends upon the ability, the machinery, the capital employed, and the intentions, as to who wins: Government, who represents the interests of the whole people, or the individual contractors."

1151. "When you first set up your factory here, did you send for machinery from America?"—"No, I first began to buy it here, but it would not do, and I sent to America for it; it was not made for small work. You make a very nice large machine here, but when you come to little details for making fire-arms, I do not know a man competent to do it. Mr. Whitworth comes nearest of those I have met, but he has not made me a good machine yet, nor a perfect machine for my business; he does not make gun machinery; he has not begun to make it. He is, I presume, competent to do it, or any thorough workman, but he has not done it with perfection enough to make guns to interchange."

1152. "Had you much trouble with your men here at first?"—"I had a good deal of trouble to start with. I found great difficulty in this: I brought over first some Americans here, to lead off as my master workmen, but the climate and the habits of the people did not agree with them; they left the jobs. I began here then by employing the highest-priced men that I could find to do different things, but I had to remove the whole of those high-priced men. Then I tried the cheapest I could find, and the more ignorant a man was, the more brains he had for my purpose; and the result was this: I have men now in my employ that I started with a two shillings a day, and in one short year's time I cannot spare them for eight shillings a day; I pay some few of them that, and I would not let them go just now if they required nine shillings. That is the result of employing your men of ignorance. They first come as laborers, at two shillings a day, and, if I find them expert and honest, I employ them as watchmen, or to weigh metal. In a little time, if there be a machine vacant, I put them on it. They would improve from two shillings in the first few months up to four shillings or five shillings, and by and by they become masters. One-half of my masters are Englishmen now, and they fill the vacancies of the Americans who become dissatisfied, from ill-health and from other causes, and go home. The best get eight shillings a day, and at last they become masters too. Do not bring me a man that knows anything, if you want me to teach him anything."

1153. Mr. Walpole. "You want good brains, and little knowledge?"—"Yes, I take the raw material."

1154. Mr. Newdegate. "Do you mean that you can get more undivided attention from such men?"—"Yes, the more lessons you can teach them. Take a man here that has been in the habit of rifling a barrel, and he will not do it in any other way than he has been used to do it; but take the raw material, and bring him up to the work (and you have millions of it here), promote the man, and put him in the line of promotion, and he will produce the result you want, and he is elevated."

1170. Mr. Geach. "You have a patent for your pistol; it was taken out in 1836, was it not?"—"Yes; and several for improvements since."

1171. "You were induced to open your establishment for the purpose of carrying the work to perfection, and getting the largest amount of profit that you could out of it?"—"Yes; and I am now proud of the results of my exertions, and can paddle my own canoe."

1172. "It was not, I think, until 1850 that you were enabled to derive the full benefit of the patent?"—"I was not successful here at all; I had to devote all my energies at home."

1173. "I am speaking of America now: until 1849 or 1850, even in America you were not successful, and you made no profit?"—"It was not profitable; I did not make any money till lately; I made none in America until my arms were employed in the service, by the energy of the people who went first to Florida, next to Texas, in the wars against the Indians, and finally to Mexico, in our war with that country; that completed the reputation of my arm so far as America is concerned. After the Mexican war commenced, its peculiarities being known, the arm, which I was selling to the Government at twenty-five dollars apiece, was sold by individuals and soldiers as high as two hundred dollars to traders; and such was the desire to get those arms, that officers sometimes bought from the traders at those large prices for their own private use, without a knowledge where those arms came from."

1174. "Do you mean your pistol?"—"Yes; my pistols were sold usually for from about seventy-five to one hundred and fifty dollars, and sometimes two hundred dollars each; and the tradesmen resold them to our own officers when the Government paid me only twenty-five dollars."

1175. "In 1847 you had a contract with the Government, had you not?"—"Yes; immediately after the war commenced, then the Government came to me for the arms. The other arms which I made originally got into the service; and when I recommenced my manufacture I advertised in the newspapers for a specimen of my own arm, as I had given my samples and models all away to friends; but I did not find one at the time; and in getting up the new ones I made improvements on the old."

1176. "In 1847 you took a contract for one thousand of those pistols from the Government?"—"Yes."

1177. "For twenty-four thousand dollars?"—"Twenty-eight thousand the first contract, and twenty-five thousand afterwards; the last price was twenty-four dollars each."

1178. "Those one thousand you stated, did you not, cost you twenty-seven thousand dollars to make?"—"I lost by the first thousand; and the reason was, that I had to get machines to make the arms even possible, and I ran my machinery night and day."

1179. "You found that it was some time before you got your machinery to that perfection to which you have raised it now?"—"Yes, it was; I not only improved upon the machinery, but in the model of the arm itself, the same arm for which I contracted, and the result was much better for both the Government and myself."

1189. "Supposing that, instead of private individuals furnishing the money, you had been supplied with the one hundred and fifty thousand dollars that you lost in the first instance by the Government, and they had refused to give any more money, that would have been a failure, would it not?"—"Yes, it was a failure any how; I had to pay thirty thousand dollars out of my own pocket for this failure of private enterprise in making my arms: it is not very creditable to me to have my arms fail under any circumstances, but they did fail; the facts are known to everybody; I have gone to work individually, and I have succeeded by my individual energy and the circumstances of the times."

1214. "What is the price at which you have supplied those arms to the Government?"—"I supply them for any thing I can get."

1215. "What have you supplied them to the Government for?"—"I do not choose to tell you; the Government will answer that question for themselves; I will tell nobody what I supply my arms for. If you want to buy, and say you will buy ten thousand of them, and will give me a fair price, you can have them to-day."

1216. "How are we to estimate the cost of making the machinery by your process, if you will not tell us the price at which you make the article?"—"I will not tell you the price."

1235. "Will you be good enough to state when you commenced the erection of your establishment?"—"The instant I got home, after I had ordered an engine here, which the contractors agreed to furnish in six weeks' time, I made one lot of machinery in America to come here; I put the first lot of machinery in my own American manufactory, and I made a second lot of machinery, and that machinery I also put to work there; this was all done since I left, and since the great World's Fair. After putting the two lots of machinery to work at home, I wrote constantly to know when my engine ordered here would be done, and they said, six weeks after the operatives went to work again. I came here with a third lot of machinery made to start this fabrication, and I waited three months before I got the engine going."

1239. "My object in putting the question is to ascertain how long it is probable the Government here will be in completing a manufactory, by ascertaining how long you had been?"—"That depends on how smart the Government is."

1263. "There is a great difference between your own pattern and the musket on the table, is there not?"—"I should say that I was not competent to make my own, if I could not make such a thing as that."

1264. "The first cost of the first fifty thousand would be greater than that of the next fifty thousand, would it not?"—"Yes; I would not undertake to make one hundred and fifty thousand arms without an extra pound, because so much money must be sunk in machines and fixtures to get fairly started."

1265. Colonel Dunne. "In adopting your pistol, have not the Government been satisfied with the shape of your arm, and not bound you to any difficult machinery?"—"They have taken it, generally; they admit that my test was pretty good."

1266. "Do not you think they would do the same as to muskets?"—"A musket is an old established thing; it is a thing that has been the rule for ages; but this pistol is newly created; there is nothing that cannot be produced by machinery; if it is necessary to make that hammer (pointing to the same) in that particular form, it can be done.

Chapter Four

THE COLT REVOLVER

By J. D. Butler, *Professor of the State University of Wisconsin*

The Parts of the Colt Revolver

A revolving pistol consists essentially of, 1st, The Barrel; 2nd, The Cylinder; 3rd, The Lock-frame (containing the lock); 4th, The Stock.

1. The barrel is made of steel and is rifled. It is in all respects like the barrel of any muzzle-loading arm, except that it is open at both ends, and on its lowest side are a socket for the rammer, and the fixtures for fastening the rammer and its lever to the barrel. These fixtures are all forged in one piece with the barrel. There is also a slot below for holding the key of the cylinder-pin, hereafter described.

2. The cylinder is a piece of steel in which five or six chambers parallel to the axis are bored. Their bore and that of the barrel are the same. They are open to the front, and stop at a distance from the rear of the cylinder great enough to leave sufficient metal behind the chamber to give proper security against bursting. Behind each chamber, and entering it, an orifice is cut, which the screw on the base of the cap-cone fits, so that the cone is fixed directly in rear of the chamber.

Besides the chambers, there is another hole in the cylinder whose axis is the axis of the cylinder, and which is bored entirely through it. Through this, and fitting it precisely, passes a pin from the lock frame to the barrel. The pin is parallel to the bore of the barrel, and so far below it that the revolution of the cylinder brings in succession each chamber directly behind the barrel, so that the chamber and bore of the barrel can be made continuous. This pin secures the cylinder in position between the lock-frame and barrel, allowing it only to revolve about its axis. It is secured to the barrel by a key passing through a slot cut in the pin, and a corresponding one in the barrel.

On the rear of the cylinder is cut a ratchet, having 5 or 6 teeth, as the cylinder has five or six chambers. The centre of the ratchet is on the axis of the cylinder, and the teeth are so arranged, that when the piece is at full cock a chamber is directly in rear of the barrel.

On the surface of the cylinder are cut as many small slots as there are chambers. The lowest of these slots is entered by the end of a bolt, which is movable by the action of the lock, and is pressed into the slot by a spring constantly acting. So long as the bolt is in the slot, the cylinder is immovable.

3. The lock-frame is directly in rear of the cylinder, and consists of the recoil-piece, into which the cylinder-pin is fastened; the lock, which contains the machinery for exploding the cap, as well as revolving and locking the cylinder; and a frame, which contains and holds in place the mainspring.

In the lock the sear and trigger are in one piece, as are also the hammer and the tumbler. In these respects the lock differs from that used before the invention of the revolver by Colt. The mainspring acts upon the tumbler and hammer directly.

The tumbler has fastened on its face a "hand," which engages the ratchet on the rear of the cylinder, and is held against it by a spring. It also has a projecting pin, which is so arranged that at the proper time it engages the bolt which locks the cylinder, lifting it out of its seat in the cylinder-slot, and giving it freedom to move under the action of the "hand." When the pin no longer acts upon the bolt, the spring, which constantly acts upon it, forces it into the first slot which it meets in the revolution of the cylinder, thus locking it.

The action of the lock is as follows. The hammer is supposed to be resting upon one of the cap-cones.

The hammer being slightly raised, there is at first no motion of any part, except that of compression of the mainspring. This device is used to permit any pieces of exploded caps to fall out at the raising of the hammer, before the other parts are in motion. The raising of the hammer being continued, the pin in the face of the tumbler, disengages the bolt from the slot in the cylinder; immediately afterwards the "hand" engages a tooth of the ratchet, and as the hammer is raised the cylinder is revolved by the "hand" one-fifth or one-sixth of a revolution, according as there are five or six chambers. When the hammer arrives at the full cock, the tumbler-pin is disengaged from the bolt, which flies back into the cylinder-slot by the action of its spring, and bolts the cylinder. The piece is then ready for discharge, and the cap can be exploded by pulling the trigger.

4. The stock, composed of wood or ivory, is immediately in rear of the lock, and embraces that part of the lock-frame which contains the mainspring. It forms the handle or grip.

The piece is loaded by inserting the powder and ball or cartridge in the front ends of the chambers. These are successively brought under the rammer, and the loads are pressed home by the action of an ingenious lever arrangement attached to the barrel and worked by the hand. The piece is then capped, when it is ready for discharge.

Although, in the various forms and models of revolving arms made since the date of Colt's inventions, there have been some deviations from the details of this description, the principle of the arm is in all of them the same as that given here.

Varieties

THE TEXAS PISTOL, as it was at first named, was made at Paterson, New Jersey, about 1838. It was the first form of revolver which came at all into general use, and was a popular arm along the Western frontier. Its calibre was .34. It had a concealed trigger, which was thrown out by the act of cocking, was without a guard, and had no lever attachment for loading.

During the Mexican War, in 1846-'47, and '48, this pistol was in great demand in Texas and Mexico, and one hundred dollars in specie was not an uncommon price for it, even after it had been long in use.

Another pistol similar to the TEXAS ARM was also made at Paterson. It was called the Walker pistol by Col. Colt, out of compliment to a distinguished Texan Ranger of that name, with whom the pistol was a great favorite.

It was much larger and heavier than the TEXAS arm, and, although it differs in proportion of parts, was in form and arrangement very similar to the pistol known as Colt's Old Model Army Pistol.

The lever and rammer were attached to the pistol, though the idea of a lever rammer was suggested by sketches of a much earlier date. Its calibre was 44.

THE OLD MODEL ARMY PISTOL followed the Walker pistol in 1847, and was extensively introduced as a weapon for cavalry. The calibre is 44, and weight 4 pounds.

POCKET REVOLVERS, with 6 inch, 5 inch, 4 inch, and three inch barrels, and 31 bore, were introduced about 1848. They were at first made without lever rammers, and were loaded by removing the cylinder from its pin, and using the pin as a rammer.

THE OLD MODEL NAVY PISTOL, which has been the most popular of all the pistols, was introduced about 1851. It was a great advance upon its predecessors, containing an improvement in the form of cylinder-slot, which, with the bolt, secured the cylinder during discharge, making the action of the bolt more certain. This improvement was patented in 1850. The same patent also covers the safety-pins inserted in rear of the cylinder, which added much to the efficiency of the arm. Both of these improvements have been retained in nearly all of the models made since. Its calibre is 36 and weight 2 pounds 10 ounces.

THE OLD MODEL POCKET PISTOLS were improved in 1849 by

the introduction of the perfected features of the Navy Pistols, and have not been materially altered since.

Their calibre is 31 and weigh from 24 to 27 ounces, dependent upon the length of the barrel.

A small NEW MODEL POCKET PISTOL was introduced in 1855, and has an entirely different arrangement from those which preceded it. The cylinder is inclosed by a metallic frame, the trigger has a different guard, and the action of the "hand" is different.

The calibre is 31 and weight one pound. The Rifle made at this time is similar in its arrangements to this pistol.

The NEW POCKET, and NEW MODEL POLICE, NEW MODEL ARMY, and NEW MODEL NAVY have all been introduced since 1860. They present nothing new in principle, but by a better arrangement of parts, and in the Army Models by less weight, suit the markets better. The calibre, too, of the Pocket and Police pistols is 36, the same as that of the Navy pistol. The increased calibre makes them more deadly weapons. The calibre of the New Model Army Pistol is 44.

The New Pocket Pistol weighs from 25 to 28 ounces.

The New Model Police Pistol weighs from 24½ to 26 ounces.

The New Model Navy Pistol weighs 2 pounds 10 ounces.

The New Model Army Pistol weighs 2 pounds 11 ounces.

There are now made at the works fourteen models of pistols, differing essentially from each other, varying in calibre from 31 to 44, and in weight from one pound to 2 pounds 11 ounces.

The OLD MODEL RIFLES were made in Paterson in 1836-'37. They were first made to cock by a lever under the lock-frame. They were loaded by a detached lever and rammer, the end of the lever fitting into a slit in the frame, which formed a fulcrum, and the balls were pushed home by the action of the lever on the rammer. Afterwards the lever was attached to the side of the barrel, and the hammer was arranged as it is in the pistols.

Rifles for sporting purposes are now made of calibres 36, 44, and 56. In their arrangement they are like the New Model Pocket Pistol previously described. They were introduced in 1856-57 and 1858.

The barrels are of various lengths from 24 to 37½ inches.

Shot Guns of 60 and 75 calibre, and of lengths from 27 to 36 inches are made now, and are averaged like the Sporting Rifles.

Chapter Five

A VISIT TO THE COLT ARMORY IN 1863
By Henry Barnard

(Condensed from *Armsmear*)

Let us follow a bit of raw material on its pilgrimage. If it be gun-metal, that is, copper alloyed with about ten per cent of tin, its race is comparatively short. Going into the foundry, it is cast into pistol-guards and back-straps. The moulds are so made that each turns out a dozen guards at once, the molten metal flowing into a sort of tree, with guards as branches. These, when cut off, milled, filed and polished, pass to the electroplater, from whose batteries and solutions they are received by the burnishers. These brighteners now consist of ten—one man and nine girls. For their toil on each pistol, the tariff is three and one-half cents. The females daily complete about thirty sets—the man twice as many. The transformation from dull white to silvery lustre, by dint of mere friction with a steel dipped in soap and water, is astonishing.

Whenever a bar of steel or iron leaves the store-room, it starts on a long journey. It is first heated and cut on an anvil, or with shears, where the cutting is done quicker and better, into pieces short enough for convenient working. Having been again heated, it is, all in a moment, like so much wax or dough, forced into any desired shape on swage-blocks, or anvils cut in patterns. They are thus forced by hammers which, first raised by a screw rotating continuously, are then made to drop by touching a spring. They are hence named "drops." To a non-mechanical eye they seem more properly stamps than hammers, because they finish their work all at one blow—a blow so decisive and ponderous.

According as it is iron or steel, and goes to one forge to another, will it become mainspring or cone-nipple, lock-plate or lever, bullet-mould or pistol-barrel. A pistol-barrel, when stamped by the first drop, has a rude resemblance to a small dumb-bell with flattened heads. The next drop compresses one of its heads into a cylinder as narrow as its neck, leaving the other to form the barrel-shank for admitting the base-pin and ramrod lever.

The forge department is the special pride of both shops. Its machinery, mainly invented and patented by E. K. Root, the present head of the concern, is the most labor-saving, and hence dollar-saving, of all the cunning contrivances here at work. For this kind of labor there was formerly required, at each anvil, a foreman with a helper. Now the helper alone can do more than three times the work of both, and can do it better.

The apparatus for welding gun-barrels has been introduced since the rebellion broke out. All the barrels previously made, being of steel, needed no welding. In the welding process, flat bars of iron, on passing through the first groove in the rolling-machine, are "crimped," that is, hollowed, into the shape of the capital letter U. Next, they become short and thick as window weights, but are hollow, and with a slit on one side from end to end. When at a white heat, a mandril, or a sort of iron foil, with a guard to screen the workman's hand, is thrust through them, and they are rolled through an eccentric groove between iron wheels, and this squeezing is repeated a dozen times. Each time they are spitted on a thinner foil, and are rolled through a narrower groove. At the close, we behold gun-barrels in length and thickness, though of a bore strangely small. No cavity at all would be left by the elongating and compressing wheels were not the bore filled by the foils, which withstand outside pressure. The two sets of rollers can each furnish forth a hundred barrels in a day.

No words can paint any adequate picture of the gauntlet a musket-barrel runs. Yet that its career is long and hard, will be apparent from a list of some few of the operations for which names have been coined. The moment it emerges from the welding-jaws it is plunged for an instant in water, and, while still red-hot, it is straightened on the outside, being laid in a steel couch . . . next it is cut off of the right length . . . It then has a cone-nipple, for holding the percussion cap, inserted into its side. Having been annealed, that it may be softer for tools, it is nut-bored on a boring-bank, that is, a rod, being thrust through it, has a nut fastened on its end, and is gradually pulled back again, so as to enlarge the hole. Having next been smooth-bored by a long gimlet pushed through its whole length, and then straightened on the inside, it is fastened in a lathe and turned like a hoe-handle. Thence it passes to grinding. This work is done on Nova Scotia stones, the peripheries of which run a mile a minute. Such stones, each more than a foot thick, weighing over forty quintals, and seven feet in diameter, waste away completely, and perish within two weeks; and the barrels, but for being kept all the while wet, would shoot out brader flames than will ever burst from their muzzles. Then, sights to help the marksman's aim are brazed upon the barrel. After this long preparatory course, comes proving. The proving-house is a strong cabin in one of the courts. Thirty-two barrels stand in a stack; one man puts a tunnel in the muzzles; another pours in powder, from a cup that holds just the proof-charge; a third follows it with a roll of thick paper. Elongated balls are then put in, and pushed home with a six-pound rammer. The thirty-two are then laid in a separate room, on iron grooves nearly parallel, and pointing into a sand-bank; a train of powder is so drawn along as to unite all the touch-holes, the plank doors are shut, and the whole is exploded by a pistol. The proof-charge is about five times as much powder as one for ordinary service. The wad and ball are also heavier. Not one steel barrel in a thousand fails to bear the test; while those of iron are so much inferior, that as many as five in the thirty-two now and then burst. The place of failure is almost always at the line of welding. That sort of work gives way unless done at the very niche of time, when the metal is at exactly the just medium, neither too hot nor yet too cool. Of the 681 iron barrels lately proved, thirteen burst, and ten were condemned for other faults, so that about one in thirty of them were failures.

It sometimes so falls out, that the proof-charge which will not rend a barrel, will so far weaken the metal that it will fly asunder the next time it is fired, even with a smaller charge. To ascertain whether this is the case, the barrels are tried again, with a charge one-fifth lighter than at first. But it is found that very few that stand the first test prove unequal to the second. As has been said, a thousand steel barrels are proof against the larger charge, where one fails, Hence, the prospect of a flaw in a steel barrel, which has endured the first proof, is too slight to rouse much interest in firing it the second time.

Doubtless it is wise to guard against all possibilities. An ordinary day's work for two men, aided a trifle by the United States inspector, will prove about 256 pieces—for each which they are paid one cent.

An accepted barrel must be "counter-bored" in the breech . . . Counter-boring is a cut round the head of an orifice, the sides of which are perpendicular to that orifice, instead, as in counter-sinking, of being beveled down to it. The would-be barrel is next "tapped" with shallow holes, like a sugar-tree. It is then "milled," for squaring or angling the breech. It is "jigged" on its cone-seat.

The operation which follows is of special nicety, and is termed reaming. It is thrice repeated, and performs for the inside of the barrel what polishing afterwards effects for its outside. A wedge of thin paper is here of power to cause a piece to be accepted or rejected . . . It is next to be polished. A machine does this service, except that it leaves a few inches at each end to be finished by hand. The value of machines is here brought to view. One machine polishes two hundred barrels a day throughout five-sixths of their length. No less than fourteen men must be busy all the time to complete the single sixth which the machine omits.

Breeching up, deadening or browning, and sometimes rifling, are processes which remain before a barrel can arrive at stocking. In rifling for the United States, only three grooves are cut, and those of uniform width, though growing shallower from breech to muzzle. In those manufactured by the company on its own account, the grooves are seven, of uniform depth, but narrowing from breech to muzzle, as also with a "twist," gaining or graduated. This latter method of rifling is decidedly easier than that required by the Government, and is held by connoisseurs to be in no respect inferior. The apparatus for rifling is American in origin, of late introduction, was mostly made in the arms factory . . . Sixteen machines fashion the stock. Receiving a rough and crooked rail, they send it flying through a course of sawing, and centering, and spotting, and first-turning, and barrel-grooving, and profiling, and butt-plating, and letting in the lock, and banding, and working between the bands, and ramrod-grooving, and bedding guard and ramrod spring, and second-turning, and boring and tapping. One is at a loss to decide whether each successive process subtracts more from the weight, or adds more to beauty and adaptations. The principle of this machine is that forms are turned by a pattern having the exact shape of the object to be produced, and which in every part of it is successively brought in contact with a small friction wheel; this wheel precisely regulates the motion of chisels arranged upon a cutting-wheel acting upon the rough block, so that as the friction wheel successively transverses every portion of the rotating pattern, the cutting-wheel pares off the superabundant wood from the end of the block, leaving a precise facsimile of the model . . . The whole sixteen . . . were ordered by the British Government for their establishment at Enfield, and the very man, Mr. Oramel Clark, who now manages them here, set them up there, and managed them for more than four years . . . No operation in gun-stocking is more magical than cutting the hole for letting in the lock. A hexagonal frame, is so hung as to turn round above the stock. From each of its corners, as it halts an instant, a tool springs down fiercely, and seems to be tearing the stock in pieces. All the while a blast from two brass pipes blows away the fragments. At the end of 45 seconds, we behold, hollowed out of the solid wood, a polished cavity of five different depths, and so cunningly fashioned. . . .

The black walnut of which stocks are made, used at Springfield to be seasoned for four years. That process is here, by kiln-drying, shortened to but little more than that number of weeks. . . .

When a jigging machine has rudely scooped out the shank of a pistol-barrel, it passes into the hands of the first filer, who is paid 7 cents for each of these tubes he faithfully rubs something more into shape. His work is hard, and his pay proportionate. From him, after sundry other manipulations, it comes to the second filer. He uses seven files, costing in the aggregate $2.29, as bought of the company at wholesale, and though he cards them clean a dozen times a day, he wears out two or three sets every month. He uses them on the shank, or hook, or sight, and makes on an average twenty strokes with each. For these 140 strokes he is paid but 2½ cents; yet, as one hundred and fifty barrels daily pass through his hands, his wages are good. He stamps his initials on each, lest the inspector send back to him the bad work of another. When he screws a barrel in a vise, the jaws are faced with leather stuck on by beeswax . . . Most hammers are made from a soft alloy of tin and lead, called Babbit metal . . . Including screws, there are twenty-eight pieces in a pistol, and three times as many in a regulation musket . . . It is not easy to exaggerate the readiness of interchange in the parts of a musket. So we shall judge when we have stood by the assembler, seen him pick up the pieces at haphazard, clap them together, and fasten them by eleven screws, and all within three minutes . . . Such is a meagre sketch of some of the characteristics of what may be styled the concucopia of Mars—the establishment in which fire-arms of the best model were first fabricated on a grand scale in the United States by a private company. Col. Colt lies buried near his house, in a thicket of evergreens, and beneath a plain marble slab. But his simple tomb is in full view of the arms factory, which is his true monument. Before his death, and through his energetic genius, it had become substantially what it is today. The volleys in the proving-house daily sound his requiem.

Chapter Six

U. S. WAR DEPARTMENT AND NAVY ORDERS OF COLT FIREARMS
AND PRICES PAID THEREFOR FROM 1841 TO 1857 INCLUSIVE

UNITED STATES ORDERS—WAR DEPARTMENT

1841—March 2	100 Carbines	$45	$	4,500.00
July 23	60 "	"		2,700.00
1847—January 4	1,000 Holster Pistols	28		28,000.00
November 2	1,000 " "	"		28,000.00
1849—January 8	1,000 " "	25		25,000.00
1850—February 4	1,000 " "	"		25,000.00
1851—May 8	2,000 " "	24		48,000.00
1853— " 26	1,000 " "	"		24,000.00
1855—January 15	1,000 " "	"		24,000.00
July 27	1,000 Belts "	"		24,000.00
December 6	100 " "	"		2,400.00
1856—February 13	200 " "	"		4,800.00
April 21	370 " "	"		8,880.00
" 23	125 Holster "	"		3,000.00
" 26	100 " "	"		2,400.00
" 26	100 Belt "	"		2,400.00
" 29	55 Holster "	"		1,320.00
May 3	50 " "	"		1,200.00
June 10	125 Belt "	"		3,000.00
August 14	6 " "	"		144.00
September 19	60 " "	"		1,440.00
1857—January 7	101 Rifles	50		5,050.00
" 7	500 Belt "	24		12,000.00
April 13	1 " "	"		24.00
May 13	250 " "	20.49		5,122.50
" 18	16 " "	"		327.84
June 2	100 " "	"		2,049.00
" 4	10 " "	"		204.90
" 13	200 " "	"		4,098.00
July 11	150 " "	"		3,073.50
August 12	100 " "	"		2,049.00
" 14	300 " "	"		6,147.00
" 20	200 " "	"		4,098.00
September 5	150 " "	"		3,073.50
November 3	5,000 " "	18.47 11/12		92,395.83
" 21	300 Rifles	42.50		12,750.00
	17,829			$416,567.07

NAVY DEPARTMENT

1852—July 10.........	25 Army Pistols......	$25.00...........	$	625.00
" "	50 Navy "	...... "	....	1,250.00
" "	13 6-inch "	...... 19.30...........		250.90
" "	6 5-inch "	...... 18.30...........		109.80
" "	6 4-inch "	...... 17.30...........		103.80
1856—June 16.........	50 Navy "	...... 18.64½.........		932.25
1857—May 21.........	50 " "	...... 19.43½.........		971.75
June 16.........	30 " "	...... "		583.05
August 3.......	50 " "	...... "		971.75
September 28....	1,870 " "	...... "		36,343.45
	19,979			$458,708.82

Chapter Seven

FIREARMS MANUFACTURED BY COLT'S PATENT FIREARMS MANUFACTURING COMPANY

JANUARY 1, 1856, TO DECEMBER 30, 1865

Year	Pistols	Rifles	Muskets
1856	24,053		
1857	39,164		
1858	39,059		
1859	37,616		
1860	27,374		
1861	69,655	3,193	
1862	111,676	2,287	8,500
1863	136,579	1,213	49,844
1864	10,406		46,201
1865	58,701		9,43

Chapter Eight

MANUAL FOR COLT'S REVOLVERS

The preliminary instruction in the use of the revolver should always be given on foot, but the following manual will apply equally well either on foot or mounted. In the instruction on foot the trooper should be brought to the position of Guard in the saber exercise, so as to assimilate his motions to those he will execute when mounted.

In the following manual for Colt's revolver, the term "holster" is applied equally to the holster of the saddle or its substitute on the belt.

The trooper being in position, the instructor will command: "DRAW PISTOL."

1 time, 2 motions

1. At the command, unbuckle the holster, seize the pistol by the handle with the last three fingers and the palm of the hand, the forefinger extended outside the holster, so as to be placed on the guard when the pistol is partially drawn, the thumb on the back of the handle.

2. At the command, "two," draw the pistol from the holster, placing the forefinger on the guard; raise it, placing the right wrist at the height and six inches from in front of the right shoulder; the barrel of the pistol perpendicular, guard to the front.

To load the pistol the instructor will command: "LOAD IN SIX TIMES"—1 load.

1. Place the pistol in the left hand, the little finger on the point of the key, the muzzle inclined to the left and front and upwards at an angle of sixty degrees to the horizon, half cock the pistol with right thumb, the right hand grasping the handle.

2. Let go the pistol with the left hand, turn it with the right and seize it with the left; the hammer between the thumb and forefinger, the middle finger on the guard, the last two fingers and palm of the hand grasping the handle and carry the right hand to the cartridge box and open it.

2—"HANDLE CARTRIDGE." 1 time, 1 motion.

Take a cartridge from the box with the thumb and first two fingers and carry it to the mouth.

3—"TEAR CARTRIDGE."

Tear off the end of the cartridge with the teeth and carry it opposite the chamber nearest the lever and on the side next the trooper.

4—"CHARGE CARTRIDGE." 1 time, 1 motion.

Empty the powder into the chamber and press the ball in with the forefinger, seize the end of the lever with the thumb and two first fingers of the right hand.

5—"RAM CARTRIDGE." 1 time, 1 motion.

Bring down the lever with the right hand, at the same time turning the cylinder with the thumb and forefinger of the left, until the charged chamber comes in prolongation of the lever, ram home the charge and carry the right hand to the cartridge box, leaving the lever in the charged chamber.

Repeat the above until all the chambers are charged, and after charging the last one return the lever, the thumb and two first fingers remaining on the end of it.

6—"PRIME." 1 time, 2 motions.

1. Seize the handle of the pistol with the right hand below the left, turn it with the guard to the right, muzzle to the left and front and elevated sixty degrees above the horizon, and place it in the left hand, the little finger on the right point of the key; turn the cylinder to the right with the right hand until it clicks, and carry the right hand to the cap box and open it.

2. Take a cap, press it on the exposed cone, turn the cylinder again until it clicks, and carry the right hand again to the cap box. Repeat the second motion until the priming is completed; then seize the pistol at the handle with the right hand, let down the hammer and bring the pistol to the second position of Draw Pistol.

To fire the pistol the instructor will command: "READY." 1 time, 2 motions.

1. Place the pistol in the left hand, the little finger touching the key, the muzzle to the left and front, and elevated at an angle of sixty degrees to the horizon, the guard under the thumb on the cock, the forefinger on the guard.

2. Cock the pistol with the thumb and return to the second position of Draw Pistol.

"AIM" 1 time, 1 motion.

Lower the muzzle and carry the right hand to the front of the neck, half extending the right arm, place the forefinger lightly on the trigger, close the left eye and aim horizontally.

"FIRE" 1 time, 1 motion.

Press the forefinger gradually, but quickly, on the trigger, fire and return to the second position of "Draw Pistol."

Should the instructor desire to have all the charges fired, he will give an intimation to that effect, and after bringing the trooper to the position of "Ready," he will command:

1—"AIM." 2—"FIRE."

Which will be executed as prescribed. After firing the first charge, the troopers will go through the motions of "Ready," "Aim" and "Fire," and so continue until the last charge is fired, when they will return to the second position of "Draw Pistol."

To load without observing the times and motions, the instructor will command:

1—"LOAD AT WILL." 2—"LOAD."

Load the pistol as prescribed. Prime and return to the second position of "Draw Pistol."

When the troopers execute the manual well, they will be instructed to come to the position of "Ready" as follows:

The instructor will command: "READY." 1 time, 1 motion.

Move the right hand six inches to the front, at the same time lowering the muzzle to an angle of sixty degrees with the horizon, cock the pistol with the right thumb and return to the second position of "Draw Pistol."

The trooper having been well instructed in the manual on foot, should be made to repeat it mounted, first at a halt and afterwards at the different gaits, but the progress of instruction should be slow. Every trooper should be made to execute all the motions well at each gate before passing to a more rapid gait.

Aiming, and especially at right gaits, requires some remark. Aiming should be practiced to the right, left, front and rear. In aiming to the right, left or front at a gallop, or at speed, the trooper should rise a little in the stirrups and incline the body a little to the front; the arm should be half extended, and the body turned in the direction of the object aimed at. In aiming to the rear, the right shoulder should be well thrown back and the right arm extended to its full length.

Firing should, at first, be executed with the greatest care and deliberation. The target should be 8 feet high and 3 feet wide, with a vertical and horizontal line, each an inch wide, intersecting at the height of 5 feet. The vertical line should pass through the center of the target. The troopers should be formed in front of, facing, and at a distance of 100 paces from the target. The firing should, at first, be executed at a distance of ten paces, but the distance should be gradually increased to 40 paces. A peg in front of the target will mark the point from which the trooper is to fire.

To commence the firing, the instructor will cause the trooper on the right to move five paces to the front, turn to the right, move 30 paces to the front, turn to the left, move to the front until he arrives abreast the peg in front of the target, then turn to the left and move to the front until he comes opposite the target, turn towards it, cock the pistol, aim and fire deliberately; then turn to the left, move 30 paces to the front, turn to the left again and pass to the rear of the troop, reload and take his place on the left of the rank.

To fire to the right the trooper executes what he did in firing to the front, except that he does not turn towards the target when he comes in front of it. To fire to the left the instructor causes the trooper on the left to execute, inversely, what the trooper on the right executed in firing to the right. To fire to the rear, the trooper on the right executes what he did in firing to the front, except that he turns from the target instead of towards it, and aims to the rear. The points where the troopers are required to turn in the exercise will be marked by pegs.

At first but one chamber of the pistol should be discharged by each trooper, and great care should be taken to guard against frightening the horses. The troopers should be cautioned to be gentle with them and soothe them when excited. When a young horse is very timid, he should be accompanied by one which has courage. When the troopers are sufficiently instructed in the exercise, and control their horses well, three or more targets should be used. They should at first be placed on the same line, and 100 paces apart; but the distance should be gradually reduced to 50 paces.

CHAPTER NINE

LETTER TO SAMUEL COLT'S SON BY I. W. STUART

Isaac W. Stuart presented Samuel Colt's son, Samuel Jarvis Colt, with a canoe-shaped cradle made of the wood of the Charter Oak tree and wrote the following letter of presentation.

Colt then lived at "ARMSMEAR." That name, given by Colt to his home, derives its meaning from the change made by Colt "ARMS" in the "MEAR." MEAR is the old Saxon word for meadow or brad field.

Master Sam. Jarvis Colt:—

You are a tiny infant now, Sammy, just bursting into life, and cannot read or understand what I write you at the present time. But you will grow, and be able to read and understand it by and by, and then you will find out that a friend of your father and mother and to you, sent for your use this day a beautiful present—a cradle for you to rock in when you were a baby, and a cradle made from the wood of a very famous tree called the Charter Oak.

This tree is famous, Sammy, because a long, long time ago, when the State in which you were born was as young almost as you are now, a very bad man, named Edmond Andros, came with a troop of soldiers to the town in which you first saw the light, and tried to take away from the good people there, a long parchment roll which was called the Charter of Connecticut.

Now, this Charter made the people of whom I speak a very free people. It gave them liberty, and liberty, you will live, I hope, to learn, Sammy, is a very precious thing, and ought to be defended at the cost of all the money in the world—yes, and at the cost, too, sometimes, even of human life.

But the people of whom I speak were few in number and weak, and no match at all in power for that man who came to take away their Charter, for this bad man was backed by a great tyrant king, who lived far way across the rolling sea, and who had armies and navies big enough to crush the little settlement in which these people lived, forever. So Edmond Andros thought he was sure of getting the Charter, because these people were weak, and he and his master were strong; and he went, therefore, with a file of soldiers into a large room, called the Court Chamber, where the Governor and Deputy Governor, and the great men of these people were assembled—there he went to take the Charter. But just as he moved forward to a large round table on which the Charter lay, and was stretching out his hand to snatch it, the candles in the chamber were all suddenly blown out, as quick as thought, and a very brave, patriotic man, named

Captain Joseph Wadsworth, who loved the people and the liberty of which I speak, seized the Charter itself, in the midst of the darkness, and running with it as swift as a deer, just as you will run, I hope, by and by, Sammy, he hid it in the hollow of a beautiful great oak; and when the candles in the chamber where Edmond Andros was, were lighted up again, lo, Sammy, the Charter was gone! And Andros couldn't find it anywhere, and never did, and the people of whom I speak were happy again, and rejoiced because their liberty was saved by means of this beautiful great oak; and they loved this oak forever after.

Now, Sammy, your cradle is made out of the wood of this beautiful great oak, and it should teach you always to remember that hero who hid the Charter so well, and make you follow his example in defending your country whenever it is in danger. Die for your native land, Sammy, rather than let anybody hurt it!

This cradle too should teach you to be wise, and virtuous, and honorable, and industrious, just as those good men were who lived when the oak was made so famous. They thought it was best always to do right—so always think yourself. They adored liberty—so do you always adore liberty. They worshipped justice—so do you always worship justice. They made truth their idol—so do you always make truth your idol. They worked out their own prosperity—in other words, these good men of the olden time "paddled their own canoes." So always do yourself; and mark it, Sammy, that I caused your cradle to be made in the shape of a beautiful canoe, in order to remind you of this sterling duty. Your father thought a great deal of this duty, and he acted it out, and once told a committee of the lofty British Parliament that "he paddled his own canoe." Sammy, remember this!

But first, and last, and best of all, my little friend, those good men of whom I speak, who lived in the days when that oak of which your cradle is made first became famous, loved God, that great and good being above us, far away up in the golden skies, who takes care of us all, and wants us to love him, and if do so, will make us all happy. Sammy, love God, love your father and mother, love your Aunt Hettie, who is all the time now finding pretty dimples in your cheeks; love all your kindred, love all mankind. "Be virtuous," Sammy, as your father often says, and then you will certainly be happy, and go some day and see God.

From the old proprietor of the Oak,

And your true friend,

I. W. STUART

Chapter Ten

ON THE DEATH OF SAMUEL COLT

By L. H. Sigourney

And hath he gone, whom late we saw
   In manly vigor bold?
That stately form and noble face
   Shall we no more behold?
Not now of the renown we speak
   That gathers round his name,
For other climes beside our own
   Bear witness to his fame;

Nor of the high inventive power
   That stretched from zone to zone,
And 'neath the pathless ocean wrought,
   For these to all are known;
Nor of the love his liberal soul
   His native city bore,
For she hath monuments of this
   Till memory is no more;

Nor of the self-reliant force
   By which his way he told,
Nor of the Midas-touch that turned
   All enterprise to gold—
And made the indignant River yield
   Unto the osiered plain—
For these would ask a wider range
   Than waits the lyric strain;—

But choose those unobtrusive traits
   That dawned with influence mild,
When in his noble mother's arms
   We saw the noble child,

And noted, mid the changeful scenes
   Of boyhood's sports or strife,
That quiet, firm, and ruling mind
   Which marked advancing life.

So, onward as he held his course
   Through hardship to renown,
He kept fresh sympathy for those
   Who cope with fortune's frown—
The kind regard for honest toil,
   The joy to see it rise,
The fearless truth that never sought
   His frailties to disguise—

The lofty mind that all alone
   Gigantic plans sustained,
Yet turned unboastfully away
   From fame and honors gained;
The tender love for her who blest
   His home with angel-care,
And for the infant buds that rose
   In opening beauty fair.

Deep in the heart whence flows this lay
   Is many a grateful trace
Of friendship's warm and earnest deed
   Which naught can e'er replace;
For in the glory of his prime
   The pulse forsakes his breast,
And by his buried little ones
   He lays him down to rest.

And thousands stand with drooping brow
   Beside his open grave,
To whose industrious, faithful hands
   The daily bread he gave—

The daily bread that wife and babe
  Or aged parent cheered,
Beneath the pleasant cottage roofs
  Which he for them had reared.

There's mourning in the princely halls
  So late with gladness gay—
A tear within the heart of love
  That will not dry away—
A sense of loss on all around,
  A sigh of grief and pain;
"The like of him we lose today,
  We may not see again."

LYDIA HUNTLEY SIGOURNEY

CHAPTER ELEVEN

DID COLT INVENT THE REVOLVER?

By MARTIN RYWELL

Did Samuel Colt invent the revolver? Invention breeds claimants. The problem of designing a gun that would shoot more than once without reloading was an ancient one. We know that the answer was attempted as early as the 16th century. Its principle was to bind together several handguns. Other attempts were made with several barrels, several loads in a single barrel, or with a cylinder with several holes as barrels.

The multishot weapons revolved manually. A catch locked the barrels with a nipple under the hammer and pull upon the trigger guard released the catch. Ingenious mechanisms were devised. Thus we find attempts at solution that began with matchlock ignition and continued through wheel-lock and flintlock. These ignition systems in common depended upon a spark ignition of the priming powder outside of the chamber. This made possible the ignition and explosion of more than one chamber simultaneously. Percussion ignition was the solution. The basic principles of multi-shot had already been developed. Percussion ignition sanctioned their safety.

Samuel Colt claimed cylinder rotation by cocking the hammer but based upon percussion ignition. Colt arrived just at the right time because percussion was the answer. His patent of February 25, 1836, gave us the revolver.

Professor Henry Barnard in Armsmear writes:

"In the year 1830, on a voyage to Calcutta, as a sailor before the mast, Samuel Colt whittled out of a ribbon-block the first model of the cylinder of his revolver and reduced to a tangible shape parts of the machinery by which the weapon was made effective. In the Summer and Fall of 1831 he constructed at Hartford his first two pistols, one of which burst upon the first trial. In 1832 he deposited a description of his invention in the Patent Office at Washington; and in 1833 constructed in Baltimore both a pistol and rifle on the same principle which was patented in England and France in 1835 and in the United States February 25, 1836."

The U. S. Patent Office in reply to our inquiry as to the 1832 description being filed, replied: "We regret that we are unable to inform you as to whether or not Samuel Colt filed a description of his invention in the year 1832 in order to protect a prospective patent application, since this office does not have a record of the Caveats which were filed for the purpose of obtaining further time in which to mature inventions."

The first documentary reference to the Colt invention we have seen is a letter addressed to Samuel Colt at Baltimore and dated March, 1833, which mentions his invention. It states that his invention "was spurned at by her (step-mother) as most natural it would be." Then the letter added, "When I was in Washington I saw the same kind of pistols patented at the patent office as yours nine times at one load."

The next reference is a letter dated February 24, 1834, from Colt's father and addressed to Sam in Baltimore upon hearing that Sam was manufacturing guns of his invention. The father writes Sam, "It is possible some person has made the trial of firearms similar to the plan you describe and failed. I have an impression that a Mr. Bull, son of Deacon Bull of Hartford, six or eight years since had a plan of the kind and that after trying to introduce them in this country went to Russia with his invention but finally failed in the enterprise. If this is so I presume his plan may be seen at the Patent Office in Washington." The letter continued to give him advice about the financial exploitation of his invention.

These letters fix 1833 as the earliest mention of Sam Colt's invention and negates the story of the ship, the whittled model, and the father later having models made.

There are claimants. Were some of these claimants independent inventors and unaware of Colt's prior invention? It is possible as has happened with many an invention especially in 1836 when communication was poor.

Were these claimants actuated by jealousy. A sage once remarked "It is surprising how much good a man may do in the world if he allows others to take the credit of it."

Paul St. Gaudens wrote the author, "There is an old legend around my home section of New Hampshire that Colt got his idea for revolving arms when a young man with a medicine show that was playing Enfield, New Hampshire. The story goes that an ingenious mechanic at the Enfield colony of Shakers designed a revolving arm but his pacifistic religion prevented him from making it. So he took the drawings to Whittier, a gunsmith in Enfield Village. Whittier made several guns to the design, both shoulder and hand, and demonstrated them at the local fair where the medicine show was holding forth. Colt saw them and swiped the idea."

A search of the United States Patent Office reveals that there was an Otis W. Whittier of Enfield, New Hampshire, and that he was granted Patent No. 216 on May 30, 1837.

Whittier claims for his invention: "The nature of my invention consists of having a metallic revolving cylinder containing any requisite number of chambers, all pointing in the same direction of the barrel, affixed at the rear of the barrel, and revolving and bringing up the chambers successively in contact with the bore of the barrel for a discharge by means of a spring with a cam or pin in the end thereof, which runs in spiral grooves or channels made on the circumference of the revolving cylinder, connected with the percussion hammer, and turning said revolving cylinder by the movement of cocking the gun." It resembles the Fosbury-Webley auto-cocking revolver since the cylinder is revolved by a stud sliding a W-shaped grooves on the outside of the cylinder.

Another New Hampshire man was so convinced Colt stole the idea of the revolver from him that he had a statement to that effect carved on his tombstone. In the cemetery at West Pembroke, New Hampshire, the headstone text is as follows:

Hermon, Son of Robert and Esther Fife, Died Dec. 29, 1845. Aet. 45 yrs. and 7 mos. HERE LIES THE MAN, NEVER BEAT BY A PLAN, STRAIGHT WAS HIS AIM, AND SURE OF HIS GAME, NEVER WAS A LOVER, BUT INVENTED THE REVOLVER.

R. E. Pike in Granite Laughter and Marble Tears writes, "Pembrokians say that Hermon invented what became famous as Colt's revolver and that Colt stole the patent or plans from him." There is not any record of any patent by Hermon Fife in the United States Patent Office. The Bible says, "Jealously is cruel as the grave."

The following letter appeared in the "Tri-Weekly Kentucky Yeoman" published at Frankfort, Kentucky, on October 24, 1878.

Editors Yeoman: "Seeing that account of a curious pistol copied into the 'Yeoman' of October 10, from 'Owensboro Examiner' reminds me that there is a gentleman in Kentucky who claims privately to be the original inventor of the revolver at least seven years before Colt's invention was made known. The gentleman is Mr. William S. Shackelford, a portrait painter, now located at Paris, if my memory serves me right (and I think she does). In the summer of 1876 he was painting portraits at Wincester, and gave me a history of his life for publication in the Biographical Encyclopedia of Kentucky. He tells of some thrilling and extraordinary experiences, but with such an honest directness as to justify the belief that what he relates is strictly true. I am certain that he has remarkable mechanical genius from an inspection of many curious specimens of his handiwork, and have every reason to believe that he really did invent the revolver. Well, after many up and downs in Kentucky, his native State, he went to Athens, East Tennessee, where he lived for about two years painting portraits. Thence in 1836 he went to Knoxville as a painter and met with such success and encouragement from many prominent citizens. He says that at Knoxville he became acquainted with a silversmith named Bell, who had an Englishman working for him by the name of Titus. The latter was a splendid workman, but had no inventive genius. Bell was accustomed to import cutlery and other ware from England and on one trip returned with a revolver, a curious kind of pistol which had never been seen in America before. Instead of the cylinder now used, it was arranged with a single barrel, having a perforated ball just under the hammer which had to be turned with the hand in order to repeat the discharge.

Immediately after seeing this contrivance, Shackelford conceived the idea of causing the cylinder to revolve with the movement of the hammer. He says he worked out the invention while lying in bed at night—the same night, I think—and at once set to work making a model in wood. He completed his model in a short time and showed it to Titus, seven years before Colt's revolver was heard of. Titus saw immediately that it would make them a fortune and agreed to make a model in steel and iron, arranging to have half the profits in case it were patented. He set to work making the model when suddenly Shackelford received word that his father was dying at Lexington, Kentucky, and he was compelled to set out at once.

That was the last he ever heard of Titus or the pistol. He wrote back to Knoxville repeatedly but never heard a word from Titus who soon moved to Virginia. Shackelford never returned to Knoxville but let the matter drop on account of poverty. After his father's death he opened a studio in Lexington and then commenced modeling busts in clay also. A few years later after he was at Maysville, Kentucky, where he saw Titus land from a boat and learned that he had become immensely wealthy and supposed that he sold the model at a good figure and became rich from a partnership . . ." The letter was signed C. A. L., Lenox Collegiate Institute, Hopkinton, Iowa. October 14, 1878.

We have ascertained that Shackelford was an artist of some ability and painted a portrait of Washington in 1833. This portrait was hung in the State Representative's Hall at Frankfort, Kentucky.

The Newport, Kentucky newspaper tried their hand at some satire and on November 5, 1878 carried the following editorial signed by George M. Dittoe, Editor:

"The Inventor of The Colts Pistol—Under the above heading a correspondent of the 'Frankfort Yeoman' at the Lenox Collegiate Institute, Hopkinton, Iowa, writes: a long letter to prove that a Mr. William S. Shackelford, a former Tennessean, now a resident of Paris, Kentucky, was the 'original inventor of the revolver at least seven years before Colt's invention was made known' but that on account of poverty never got it patented.

"Now while Mr. Shackelford may have been the inventor of a like pistol, Colt never got the idea of his world-wide revolver from him. We happen to know something of that piece of business. In the town of Somerset, Ohio, there lived for the past forty years, until recently, an inventive genius by the name of Adam Hambarger, who we believe was of Pennsylvania German origin. He was a gunsmith by trade. Just prior to the issuing of the patent to Colt—a few months only, we believe—Hambarger invented and made a revolver, a five or six shooter. So proud was he of his invention that he took the instrument to the hotel of Jack Breckbill and there in that old fashioned office and bar room combined—a genuine bar, it being in one corner of the room and barred off—with its hugh fireplace in which the cracking of shell-bark hickory made all things lively even when the pure juice of the corn had overdone its work; there in that room Hambarger exhibited his invention to the crowd, all of whom thought it was a wonderful thing.

"In those days of no railroads in that part of the world, a line of coaches plied from East to West. "Breckbill's Tavern" was a point at which the coaches stopped going both ways. The coach from the West-Chilocothe, Lancaster, etc., arrived there in the evening and did not leave until the next morning.

"It so happened at the time Hambarger was showing his invention this man Colt was at the hotel, having arrived that evening from a western trip, as the register of the hotel afterwards proved. He saw, examined it closely, but said nothing. The result was that soon thereafter Colt gave to the world a patent revolver, identically the same as Hambarger's, the latter gentleman being too slow in motion to have it patented first. All the older citizens of Somerset are acquainted with the facts in the case substantially as we have related them above."

Improvements of the Colt revolver also have claimants. Manly Wade Wellman, author of an excellent biography of Wade Hampton entitled, "Giant in Gray" writes:

"The Colt factory itself was glad to profit by his suggestion of an improvement for the revolver, the grooving of the cylinder to equalize explosion pressures."

Wellman explained to us, "I refer to the pattern of grooves on revolver cylinders, which, as I believe, was first suggested to the Colt factory by Wade Hampton of South Carolina. Hampton, who handled all firearms with great skill and affection, recognized the danger of the cylinder cracking at the chamber because of unequal response of the metal to the pressure of an explosion. He hit upon the use of grooves and called the factory's attention to its application. The suggestion was adopted and the Colt people sent Hampton a handsome revolver. It is possible that he used this weapon as a Confederate cavalry chief—in any case, he killed upwards of a dozen Yankees with revolver shots. Sorry, I can't give you a date, but it happened well before the War between the States, and so within the period of Colt's life and activity."

Another discussion of Hampton and Colt appears in "Butler and His Cavalry in the War of Secession." General Wade Hampton told Glenn E. Davis, "He said that before the war he used a Colt's revolver frequently in his numerous hunts. The old style of pistol then had smooth cylinders that contained the lead. On one occasion this cylinder burst when the General was shooting it. He saw that if the cylinders were grooved, the pressure when fired would be more equalized and the danger of bursting would be obviated. General Hampton then wrote to Colt, and explained fully his ideas, telling him if he agreed with him he could use the suggestion as his own. Colt patented the invention and sent General Hampton a very fine pistol specially made and thanked him for the idea."

Pirate or inventor, Colt made his name a synonym for the revolver. He who sees without understanding is only straining his eyes in the dark. "As for me," said a sage one day, "I have never come across a single person that did not bring to me something that was great." He was great himself first of all; therein lay his secret.

MARTIN RYWELL

Chapter Twelve

TABLES OF COLT ARMS
By Martin Rywell

Model	Cal.	Bbl.	Bbl. Marking	Cyl.	Cyl. Marking	Price
Holster Texas Paterson	36	4 to 6 7½ 9, 12	Patent Arms Mfg. Co. Paterson, N. J. Colt's Pt.	5s	Stagecoach Hold-up	$2500.00
Belt Paterson	31 34	4 to 6	Patent Arms Mfg. Co. Paterson, N. J. Colt's Pt.	5s	Centaur & Horsemen	$1250.00
Pocket Paterson	28 31 34	2½ to 4¾	Patent Arms Mfg. Co. Paterson, N. J. Colt's Pt.	5s	Centaur & Horsemen	$1000.00

Model	Cal.	Bbl.	Bbl. Marking	Cyl.	Cyl. Marking	Misc. & Variations	Price
Walker Dragoon	44	9"	Address Saml Colt, New York City U. S. 1847	6s	Indian & Dragoon Battle. Model U.S.M.R. Colt's Patent	No catch on loading lever. No. of Army Co. Mfgd. at Whitneyville 1847	$1500.00
Hartford Dragoon	44	7½	Address Saml Colt, New York City	6s	Indian & Dragoon Battle Colt's Patent	Shorter lever with two type catches	300.00
						2nd Model—Locking bolt face rectangular	300.00
						3rd Model—7½, 8" bbl. Cut for shoulder stock and had leaf sights	300.00
						English Model—English Proofmarks but mfgd. at Hartford	300.00
Little Dragoon	31	3 to 6 oct.	Address Saml Colt New Yor^k. City Bracket marks are at both ends	5s Held by pin	Indian & Dragoon Battle. Colt's Patent.	Straight Back Trigger Guard No loading lever	150.00
						2nd Model—Stagecoach holdup on Cyl., Round slots	150.00
						3rd Model—Has loading lever; rectangular slots	150.00
1849 Pocket	31	3 to 6" Oct.	Address Saml Colt New York City Brackets at both ends	5s 6s	Stagecoach Hold-up Colt's Patent plus number	Few 6 shot cyl.	50.00
						Wells Fargo Type 1-3" oct. bbl.—no loading lever	50.00
			Address Col. Saml Colt New York U.S. America			2nd type—Widened space bet. bbl. lug & cyl.	40.00
			Address Saml Colt Hartford Ct. Address Col. Colt London			London Colt—2 British P.M. on cyl. and bbl. lug. Address Col. Colt London	40.00
			Saml Colt				

86 HANDBOOK OF COLT GUNS

Model	Cal.	Bbl.	Bbl. Marking	Cyl.	Cyl. Marking	Misc. & Variations	Price
Navy Belt j 1851	36	7½ Oct.	Address Col. Saml Colt New York U.S. America. Address Col. Colt London	6s	Naval Battle Colt's Patent plus number	Few designed for shoulder stock. Few marked U.S. on frame or U.S.N. on butt. Type No. 1—Straight back guard; notched open top cyl. pin.	50.00
						Type No. 2—Slotted cyl. pin.	60.00
			Address Saml Colt New York City			Type No. 3—Small rd. brass guard	60.00
			Address Saml Colt Hartford Ct.			Type No. 4—Larger guard—brass or iron	60.00
			Saml Colt (215,000 mfgd.)			London Colt—P.M., rounder screw heads	70.00
Sidehammer Root Model Type No. 1	28	3⅜ oct.	Colt's Patent Address Saml Colt Hartford, Ct. U.S.A.	5s rd.	Cabin & Indian	Standard Cyl. pin	$45.00
Type No. 2	28	3½ Oct.	Colt's P't 1855 Address Col. Colt Hartford, Ct. U.S.A.	5s rd.	Cabin & Indian	Standard Cyl. pin	45.00
Type No. 3	31	3½ Oct.	Colt's P't 1855' Address Col. Colt Hartford, Ct. U.S.A.	5s fluted	Patented Sept. 10, 1850	Standard cyl. pin	40.00
Type No. 4	31	3½ Oct.	Colt's Pt. 1855 Address Col. Colt Hartford, Ct. U.S.A.	5s		m. "May 4, 1858"	55.00
Type No. 5A	28	3½ rd.	Address Col. Colt	5s	Patented Sept. 10, 1850	Standard cyl. pin	50.00
Type No. 5B	31	4½ rd.	New York, U.S.A.	fluted		m. "May 4, 1858"	45.00

Model	Cal.	Bbl.	Bbl. Marking	Cyl.	Cyl. Marking	Misc. & Variations	Price
Type No. 6A	28	3½ rd.	Address Col. Colt New York, U.S.A. Larger type than 5A & B	5s rd.	Stagecoach hold-up	Standard "May 4, 1858 V groove, end of cyl. pin	45.00
Type No. 6B	31	4½ rd.					45.00
Type No. 7	31	3½ rd.	Address Col. Colt New York, U.S.A.	5s rd.	Stagecoach	No marking and retained by screw thru cyl. rare	45.00
	31	4½ rd.					
Type No. 8	31	4½ rd.	Address Col. Colt London	5s rd.	Stagecoach hold-up (Mfgd. in Hartford)	"L" precedes No. & British P.M.	$50.00

Sidehammer Root Model 1855 common characteristics: iron; no trigger gd; stud trigger; creeping loading lever.

Model	Cal.	Bbl.	Bbl. Marking	Cyl.	Cyl. Marking	Misc. & Variations	Price
Army Holster 1860	44	7½, 8 rd.	Address Col. Saml Colt New York U.S. America	6s ¾" rebated rear	Ship scene "Patended Sept. 10, 1850"	Type 1—Fluted cyl; 7½ bbl; navy size grips	50.00
						Type 2—Civilian model—lacks shoulder stock grooves; smaller frame	50.00
			Address Saml Colt Hartford Ct.			Type 3—Cut-out and groove for shoulder stock	75.00
			Address Col. Colt London (200,000 mfgd.)			London Model	50.00
						Stamped, "U.S." and has mixes number—ARSENAL RE-ISSUE	25.00
Navy Belt 1861	36	7½	Address Col. Saml Colt New York U.S. America	6s	Ship scene	38,000 mfgd.	60.00
						Experimental: Several with fluted cylinders	60.00
Pocket of Navy Caliber 1861	36	4½ 5½	Address Col. Saml Colt, New York U.S. America	5s ⅝" rebated rear	Stagecoach Hold-up	Frame similar to 31 cal. Pocket Pistol	50.00
		6½ Oct.	Address Col. Colt, London		Colt's Patent plus no.	London Model (Hartford Mfgd.)	50.00

Model	Cal.	Bbl.	Bbl. Marking	Cyl.	Cyl. Marking	Misc. & Variations	Price
Police 1862	36	4½ 5½ 6½ rd.	Address Col. Saml Colt, New York U.S. America. Address Saml Colt Hartford, Ct.	5s Semi-fluted ⅝" rebated rear	Pat. Sept. 10, 1850	Brass trigger guards; few of iron. Frame similar to Pocket of Navy Caliber	50.00
Derringer No. 1	41 r.f.	2½ oval, flat	Colt's P. & F.A. Mfg. Co. Hartford, Ct. U.S.A. No. 1	S.S.		Button right side for lock. All metal frame. No. 1 & No. 2 originally mfgd. by National Arms Co.	75.00
Derringer No. 2	41 r.f.	2½ oval flat	Colt's Pt. F.A. Mfg. Co. No. 2	S.S.		and Bought by Colt. Mfgd. 1870 to 1890	50.00
Derringer No. 3	41 r.f.	2½ round	Colt's	S.S.		Mfgd. 1875 to 1912—snap latch Type 1—Hammer spur erect	50.00
						Type 2—Hammer spur curled	50.00
						Type 3—Larger Butt	50.00
Old Line 22 S.A.	22 r.f.	2½	"Colt's Pat. F.A. Mfg. Co., Hartford Conn., U.S.A.	7s	Unmarked cyl.	No bbl. strap; sheath trigger	25.00
1870						Type 1—Side rod ejector	50.00
						Type 2—Without side rod ejector	25.00
						Type 3—3" bbl. no ejector	25.00
						Type 4—3½ bbl. no ejector	25.00

Model	Cal.	Bbl.	Bbl. Marking	Cyl.	Cyl. Marking	Misc. & Variations	Price
House Pistol	41 r.f.	3rd	Colt's House Pistol, Hartford, Ct. U.S.A.	4s	Cyl. is shape of Cloverleaf	Has ejector rod	45.00
						Type 2—1½" oct. bbl.	40.00
Cloverleaf "Jim Fisk" 1871						Type 3—1½ rd. bbl. Brass frame. Bbl. m. "Colt" and frame m. "Pat. Sept. 18, 1871	50.00
						Type 4—2½" rd. bbl.-5s-no ejector. Rd. cyl. Bbl. m. "Patent Sept. 19, 1871, Colt's House Pistol. Hartford, Ct., U.S.A.	35.00
						Known as "Jim Fisk" because Jim Fisk of Erie R.R. murdered by this weapon.	
Army 1871 (1860 Army type)	44 r.f.	7½	Address Co. Saml Colt, New York, U.S. America	6s	Naval Battle 1.563" long Colt's Patent plus serial no	Right side-rod ejector; no groove in breech portion, Brass back strap; not cut for shoulder stock; 3½ ounces lighter than 1860 army; Transition type; about 5000 mfgd. rare	$200.00

Model	Cal.	Bbl.	Bbl. Marking	Cyl.	Cyl. Marking	Misc. & Variations	Price
1873 Peacemaker S.A. Army	45 cf	7½ rd.	Colt's Pt. F.A. Mfg. Co. Hartford, Ct. U.S.A.	6s	Half fluted	Frame marked "Pat. Sept. 18, 1871, July 2, 1872, Jan. 19, 1875, U.S." mfgd. for 68 yrs. and 360,000 produced. Ejector. 7½ bbl. calvary; 5½-Artillery; 4¾ Civilian, 3 & 4" Special	40.00
						1875-Cal. 44 r.f. Henry.	
						Hammer strikes top and not center of cartridge. 1900 mfgd.	40.00
						1878. Fron.ier Six Shooter Cal. 44-40c.f. Winchester 1885-Cal. 41 c.f., 1886-	50.00
						38 & 38-40; 1887-32 & 32-20;	
						1888-22; after 1896 designed for smokeless	40.00
New Line S.A. Pocket	41 r.f. & c.f.	2½ rd.	Colt's Pt. F.A. Mfg. Co. Hartford, Ct. U.S.A., Colt New .41."	5s	Half fluted	Frame m. "41 Cal." plus serial no.	25.00
						"PET" Model—Cal. 38 c.f. or r.f.	30.00
						"LADIES" model—Cal. 32 c.f. or r.f.	25.00
						"PONY" Model—Cal. 30 r.f. with 2¼" bbl. or 1¾" bbl.	25.00
						"LITTLE" MODEL—Cal. 22 r.f. 2⅜" bbl.	25.00

Model	Cal.	Bbl.	Bbl. Marking	Cyl.	Cyl. Marking	Misc. & Variations	Price
New Line Police & Thug S.A.	38 r.f.	2½ to 6" rd.	Colt's Pat. F.A. Mfg. Co., Hartford, Ct. U.S.A. (New Police .38)"	5s	Half fluted	Side-rod ejector and loading gate. Rubber grip with embossed representation policeman capturing thug	50.00
						Short-barrel Model—Cal. 38 c.f. or r.f.; 41c.f. or r.f.—bbl. 2¼ & 2½"—no ejector grips with police representation	45.00
Lightning D.A.	38 c.f.	2½ 3½	Colt's Pt. F.A. Mfg. Co., Hartford, Ct.	6s	⅔ fluted	Loading gate but without ejector	30.00
New Model		4½ 6 rd.	U.S.A. Colt D.A. 38.			41 c.f. Model—various bbl. lengths	30.00
						Side-rod ejector model 38 c.f.	45.00
Army D.A.	45 c.f.	7½ rd.	Colt's Pt. F.A. Mfg. Co. Hartford, Conn. U.S.A. 45 Colt	6s	⅔ fluted	Lanyard ring in butt; side-rod ejector	35.00
Frontier						Philipine Model—large trigger—6" bbl.	35.00
						Variations: 3½, 4" bbl. no ejector. 4¾, 5½, 7½ with ejector. Cal. 38-40, 44-40, 38 w.c.f., 44 w.c.f., 44 S. & W.	35.00
New Navy D.A.	38 s. & l.	6	Colt's Pt. F.A. Mfg. Co. Hartford, Ct. U.S.A.	6s	fluted	Side swing cyl.—3 & 4½ bbls. also 1892 to 1908	35.00
						1892 Model Cal. 41 s. & l. Cal. 38 s. & l.—two notches for locking bolts	35.00

Model	Cal.	Bbl.	Bbl. Marking	Cyl.	Cyl. Marking	Misc. & Variations	Price
New Army D.A.	38 c.f.	6	Colt's Pt. F.A. Mfg. Co. Hartford, Ct. U.S.A. Colt D.A. 38	6s	fluted	Side swing Cyl. 1892 1894 Model—locking lever to lock cyl. 1896 Model marked on grip 1901 Model—has oblong lanyard swivel 1903 Model—Smaller grip 1905 MARINE CORP MODEL—Frame of butt marked "U.S.M.C."	35.00 35.00 35.00 35.00 35.00 25.00
New Pocket	32	2½ 3½ 6	Colt's Pt. F.A. Mfg. Co. Hartford, Ct. U.S.A.	6s	fluted	Blue frame or nickeled; also 32 S. & W. as well as 32 1. & s. Colt	35.00
New Police	32	2½ 4, 6	Colt's Pt. F.A. Mfg. Co. Hartford, Ct. U.S.A.	6s	fluted	Target Model—6" bbl.	35.00
Bisley	45	7½	Colt's Patent F.A. Mfg. Co. Hartford, Conn. U.S.A. Bisley Model 45 Colt's	7s	½ fluted	1895 to 1912. BISLEY is English town where international target shootings held. Side-rod ejector. Bbl. 4¾, 5½ Cal. 44-40 w.c.f. 44 S. & W. Russian, 41 1. 38-40 w.c.f. 32-20 w.c.f. TARGET MODEL—Cal. 455 Eley, 44-40 w.c.f. 44 ., & W. special, 44 S. & W. Russian, 41 1., 38-40 w.c.f. 32-20 w.c.f.—7½ bbl. POCKET MODEL—3" bbl. no side rod-ejector.	100.00 75.00 40.00

Model	Cal.	Bbl.	Bbl. Marking	Cyl.	Cyl. Marking	Misc. & Variations	Price
New Service	45	4½ 5½ 7½	Colt's Pt. F.A. Mfg. Co., Hartford, Ct. U.S.A.	6s	fluted	Lanyard swivel. Side swing action. Ejector rod. 44 R. 44-40, 38-40 Cal.	30.00
						1909 U.S. ARMY MODEL	30.00
						U.S. MARINE CORPS MODEL—smaller grip and frame butt marked, "U.S.M.C."	30.00
						1917 ARMY—Cal. 45 automatic cartridge	30.00
Officers'	38	6	Colt's Pt. F.A. Mfg. Co., Hartford, Ct. U.S.A.	6s	fluted	Officers' Model Target Also used 38 S. & W., Cal. 22 l.r.	35.00
Police Positive	32	2½ 4 6	Colt's Pt. F.A. Mfg. Co., Hartford, Ct. U.S.A.	6s	fluted	Also 38 Cal. Police Positive Special bbl. 4", 5", 6" Cal. 32-20 & 38 Cal.	40.00
Camp Perry	22	10	Colt's Pt. F.A. Mfg. Co., Hartford, Ct. U.S.A.	s.s.	fluted		75.00
Detective Special	38	2	Colt's Pt. F.A. Mfg. Co., Hartford, Ct. U.S.A.	6	fluted	Identical w th Police Positive except for bbl. length	35.00
Official Police	22	6	Colt's Pt. F.A. Mfg. Co., Hartford, Ct. U.S.A.	6	fluted	Adapted for high speed cartridges	30.00
Shooting Master	38	6	Colt's Pt. F.A. Mfg. Co., Hartford, Ct. U.S.A.	6	fluted		30.00
Bankers' Special	22	2	Colt's Pt. F.A. Mfg. Co., Hartford, Ct. U.S.A.	6	fluted		30.00

Chapter Thirteen

HISTORY OF FIREARMS
By Martin Rywell

Firearms began with the discovery of gunpowder. Roger Bacon of England in 1247 wrote in an essay entitled "De Nullitate Magioe" "Take saltpetre, charcoal, and sulphur, and you can make thunder and lightning if you know how." Gunpowder is a mixture of 75% saltpetre, 15% charcoal and 10% sulphur. The charcoal burns, saltpetre accelerates the process of burning and sulphur acts as a brake. Ignited, gunpowder burns exceedingly fast, forms a large volume of gas which expands, and drives the projectile out of the gun. The ignition became the next problem of development.

The Germans claim that Berthold Schwarz, a Monk of Mayence, about the year 1330 discovered gunpowder. The legend is that he chanced to mix nitre, coal, and sulphur, was pounding them in an iron mortar, when a blow of his pestle ignited the compound.

Gunpowder was probably known earlier in the East and introduced into Europe by the Moors, because in a battle between the Spaniards and Moors in 1188, gunpowder was used.

Chinese claim to have discovered gunpowder or an explosive compound before the Christian Era. One of the Greek classics describes Alexander the Great as reluctant to attack the Oxydracae, who lived near the Indus, because the gods had lent them thunder and lightning. This was 330 years before the Christian Era.

Marcus Graecus, about the end of the eight century, directs us to pulverize one pound of sulphur, two of charcoal, and six of saltpetre in a marble mortar. Ram this powder tightly in a long, narrow tube, closed at one end, then set on fire, and the tube will fly through the air. This may be the firecracker that preceded the firearms. Hence, the history of the discovery is lost in antiquity.

As to the development of ignition, the primary conception of the serpentine probably came in the 1400's. The match-lock or a serpentine with a spring came very early in the 1500's. Match-locks were touched off by a match. The match was a piece of cord prepared to burn slowly. The two inventions, in the 16th century on the continent, of the wheel-lock and snaphaunce respectively, marked an enormous advance in the perfecting of hand firearms. They were great improvements over the earlier match-lock, but the match-lock was less costly and continued in use into the 17th century.

The wheel-lock invention was an important factor in pistol development because it enabled the gun to be carried in the holster, primed and ready for firing. The wheel-lock is alleged to have been invented in about 1517 in Nuremburg. At first it was crude in design and workmanship but it was much improved during the second half of the 1500's. Wheel-locks were so-called because fire struck out of their flints by means of a tiny steel wheel whirling around against them. It consisted of a steel wheel or disc, the edge of which, grooved and serrated, protruded through the flash pan. In the center of this wheel a square hole was cut, enabling it to be fixed to the lock plate after passing over the square cut spindle, to which the spanner or key was fitted. (See photograph of Spanner.) This spindle, passing through the lock plate, was attached by means of a short chain (usually of three links) to a very powerful spring. The wheel, when wound, was held by the nose of the sear, being forced (through a hole in the lock plate) to enter a cavity at the back of it. On pulling the trigger, the sear spring was released. This caused the wheel to revolve rapidly. The pyrites holder, by a spring, pressed upon the sliding pan cover. The pan cover was thrown back and the contact of the pyrites with the revolving wheel made sparks sufficient to fire the priming in the pan.

The snaphaunce was an early form of flintlock ignition. The hammer struck upon a piece of sulphurous pyrites. The resultant sparks fell upon priming powder in the pan and ignited it. The frizzen had a separate pan cover.

About 1630 the flintlock ignition was invented. Flint is a silica rock and produces sparks when struck on iron or steel. The sparks were delivered into the powder and discharged the firearm.

A great change came with the invention of the percussion lock in 1805 by the Reverend Alexander Joseph Forsyth, Presbyterian Parish minister of Belhelvie, Aberdeenshire, Scotland. His patent was issued July 4th, 1807, though it did not come into general use until the second quarter of the 19th century.

This Scotch clergyman dabbled in chemistry as a hobby. He saw the possibilities of the detonating qualities of fulminate of mercury. Percussion or detonating means capable of instantaneous explosion when struck. The hammer strikes the detonating mixture which ignites the gunpowder. Reverend Forsyth invented a gun lock in which a minute quantity of fulminate of mercury exploded when struck by the hammer and fire was transmitted through the vent to the gunpowder.

This invention was epoch making because until then all guns were fired by a flame outside the gun. Percussion led to ignition within the gun. It employed a chemical principle rather than fire. It was quicker than flintlock. It eliminated loose priming powder. It was the basic principle of the metallic cartridge and led to its development. It led to the development of smokeless powder. It gave Samuel Colt the means to perfect the revolver.

Chapter Fourteen

ETYMOLOGY OF FIRE ARM TERMS

By Martin Rywell

ARQUEBUSE—is German for "bowed or hooked box." In German, a gun is a "fire-box." (See Cannon.)

ARTILLERY—comes from the stem of the word "art" or the degree of skill to manage that branch of military science.

BLUNDERBUSS—is a corruption of "thunder-box." (See Arquebuse.)

CANNON—means a large reed or cane. The stock originally formed a straight line with the barrel. (See Arquebuse.)

DAG—short form of the word dagger denotes a short and early form of the wheel-lock pistol. It had a short flat stock. Used principally during the late 1500's.

FALCON—an ancient piece of ordance. (See Musket.)

FIRE-ARM—is an arm that produces fire.

GUN—abbreviated from "engine," a term for all larger firearms except mortars.

MUSKET—originally meant a "hawk." Invented when falconry was in flower, it could bring its victims from the air as the hunting hawk. (See Falcon.) During the 1600's a forked rest was used with the musket by unmounted men. Mounted men fired from the hip.

PETRONEL—a corruption of poitrinal, the name originally used by the French to describe the early bombardes. The term petronel was used later for the long, straight pistols used by the cavalry at the end of the 1500's.

PISTOL—the earliest use in English of the word pistol was in 1575 in a statue. The word, "dag," the early form of the word dagger was used as synonymous with pistol. Therefore, pistol could have at first meant a bludgeon or pounder. Pistols are said to owe their name to Pistoia, an Italian city, where hand-guns were fabricated. Some etymologists believe that pistol is an offshoot from the same root with piston and pestle.

CHAPTER FIFTEEN

ILLUSTRATIONS

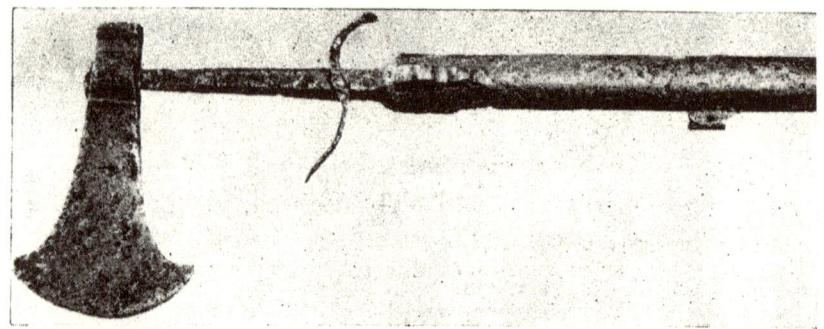

COMBINATION BATTLE-AXE AND MATCH-LOCK PISTOL, circa 1400's

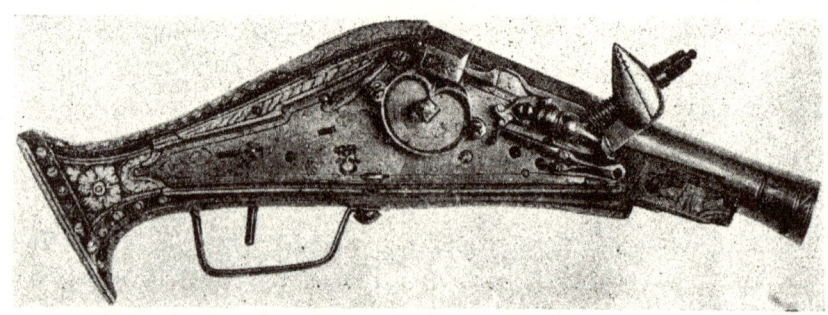

WHEEL-LOCK DAG, circa late 1600's

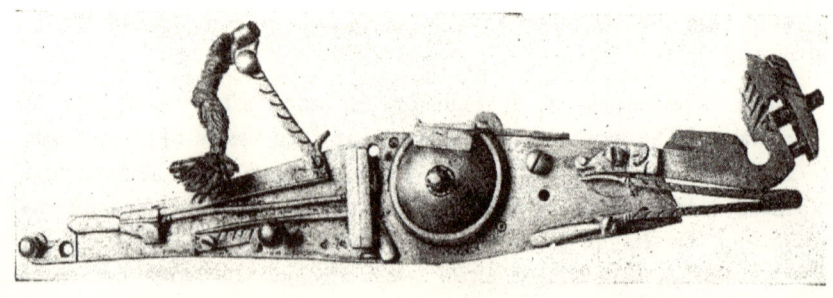

COMBINATION WHEEL-LOCK AND MATCH-LOCK circa 1600's

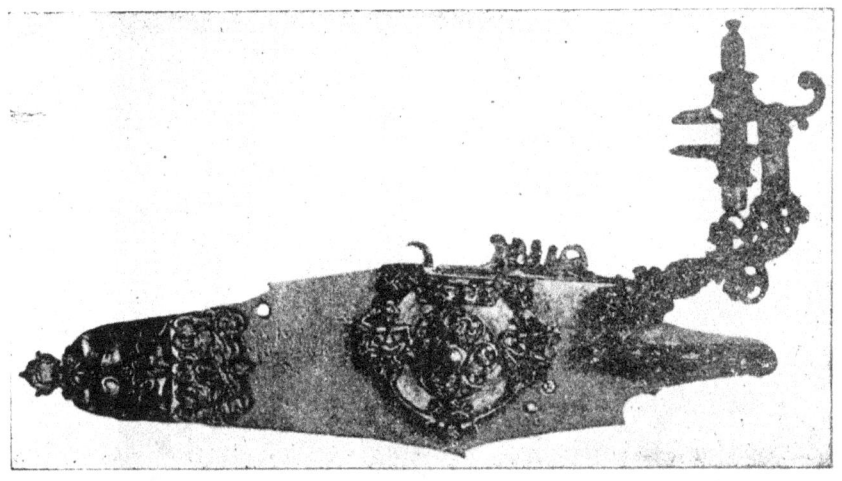

WHEEL-LOCK (made in Brescia)

WHEEL-LOCK WITH GEARED WHEEL circa 1600's

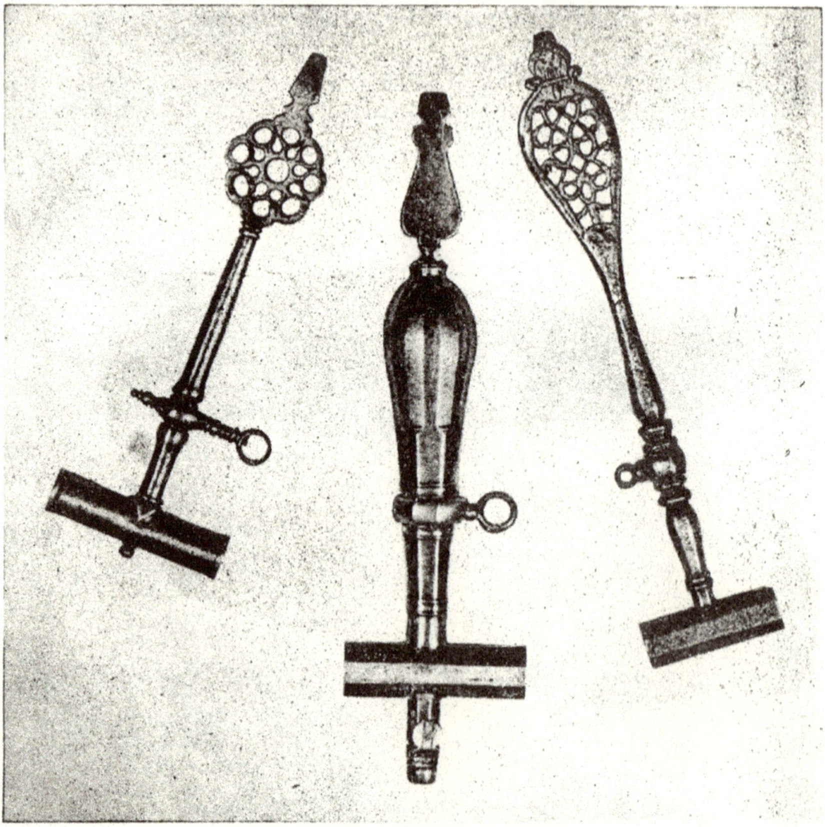

TWO SPANNERS: A COMBINED SPANNER AND PRIMER. Used to wind wheel-lock.

SNAPHAUNCE LOCK, early type

FINELY CHISELLED LOCK, 1600's, made by Lazarino Cominazzo of Brescia.

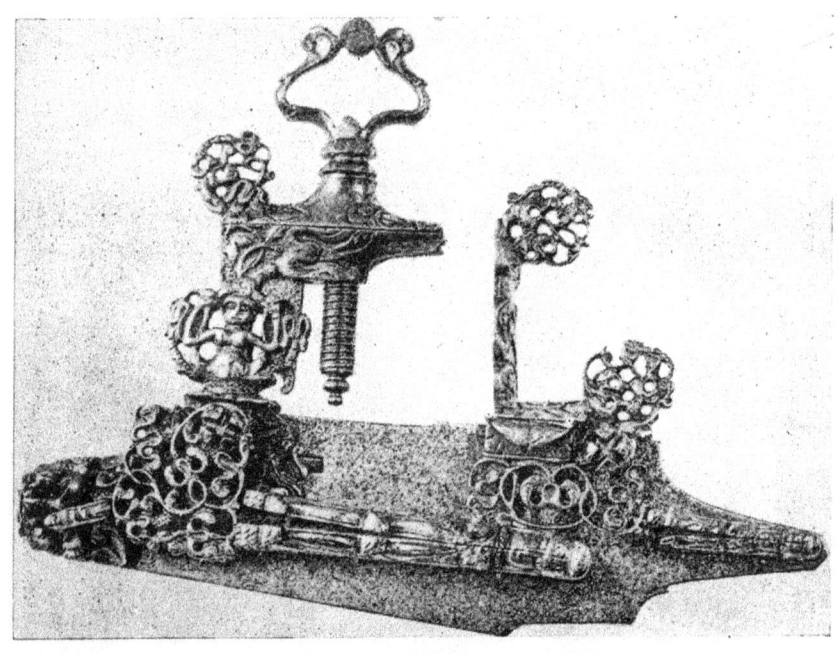

EARLY FLINT-LOCK, circa 1600's (Spanish)

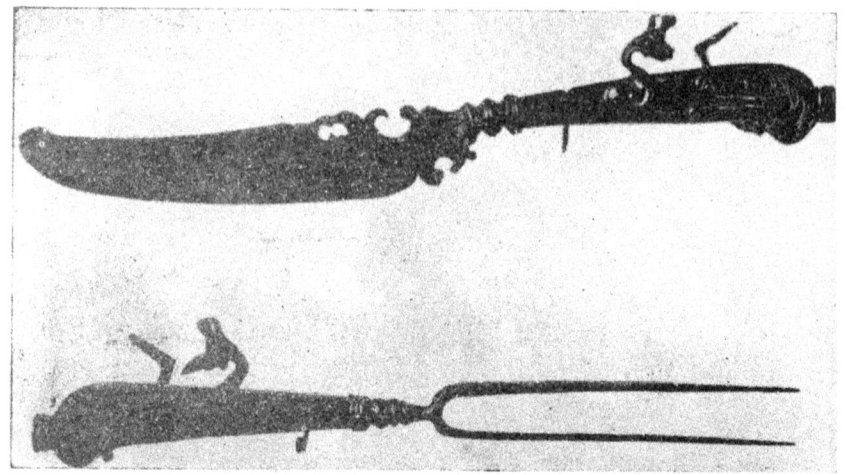

KNIFE AND FORK: THE HANDLES ARE FLINT-LOCK PISTOLS.

ITALIAN FLINT-LOCK

4-barrel pistol and single barrel pistol. Hand-revolved 4-barrel pistol by Segallas-London. Upward pressure on back of trigger guard releases the catch which retains barrels in position.

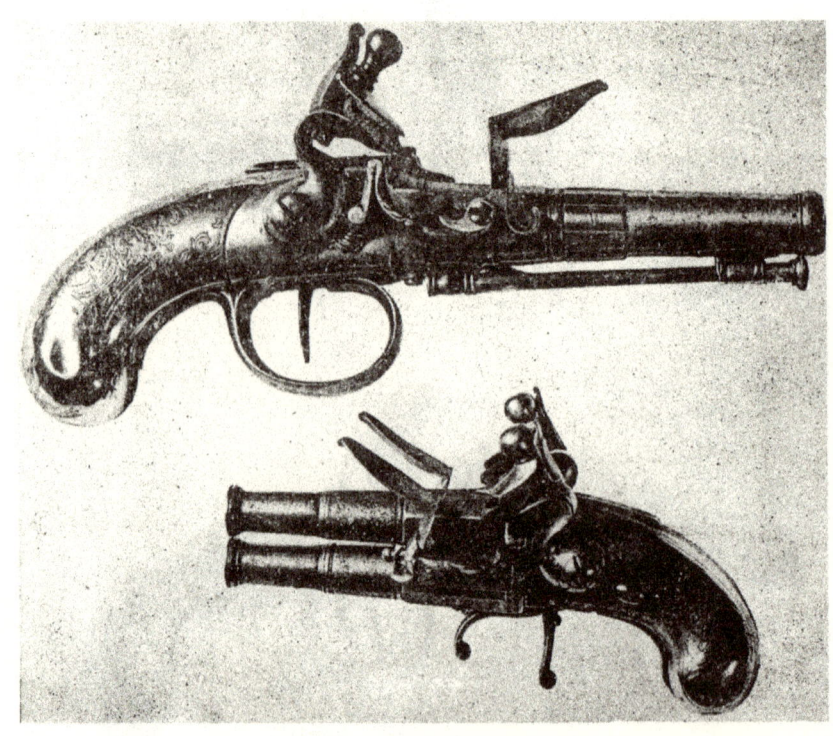

Single; Double-barrel Pistols

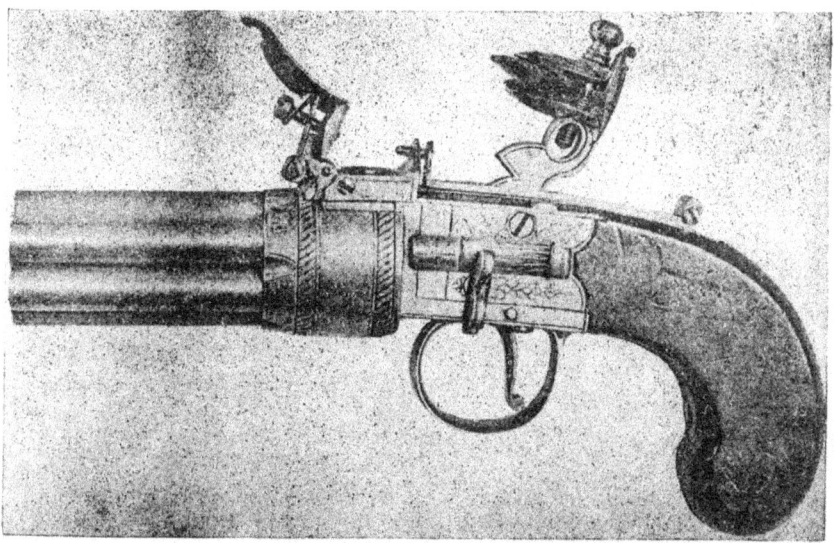

SEVEN-BARREL FLINTLOCK REVOLVING PISTOL

English made by Hunter 1750. Hand revolved. A spring and turnscrew regulate the catch that retains barrels in position. Two barrels (under the flash pan and center one) fire simultaneously when bolt attached to lock plate is pushed in. The other five barrels fire separately.

HUNTING SWORD WITH FLINT-LOCK PISTOL ATTACHED

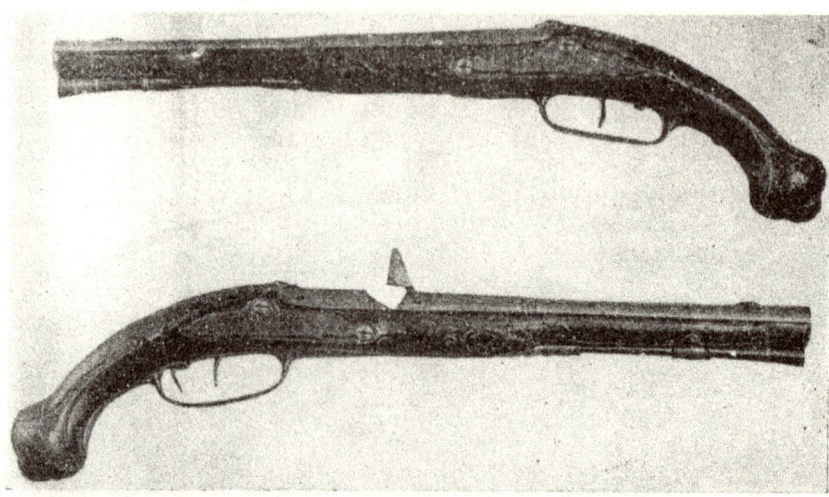

HAMMERLESS PISTOL (FLINT HOLDER IN BARREL)

Hammerless introduced about 1700's. In Tower of London is one marked, "Stanislaus Paczelt-1738." The doghead of above hammerless is attached to a spiral spring within the breech-end of barrel. The steel is the face of the triangular wedge and below is flash pan. When the trigger is pulled, the spiral spring is released and causes the flint-holder to strike the steel and fire the primer in the pan.

4 CHARGES FROM ONE-BARREL PISTOL

The charges are rammed one on top of the other. Two locks on each side so placed that their flash pans correspond exactly with touch holes equidistant along the barrel. The danger was in pulling the wrong trigger since they had to be fired in rotation.

SCREWLESS LOCK—OPERATED BY MOVEABLE PLATE

EARLIEST DETONATING IGNITION LOCK—marked J. Gutierrez, Sevila, 1720.

Spanish invention with striker shaped as a dog is attached by a connecting rod to the magazine. The top of the magazine shaped as a rabbit squatting. At full cock the magazine contains the detonating powder and is above the touch hole. When the trigger is pulled, the magazine slides back and leaves sufficient detonating powder in the small pan to be fired by the striker. The screw in the middle of lock is hollow and forms the touch hole.

COMBINATION FLINT AND PERCUSSION LOCK
Lock marked Ezekiel Baker 1821; by means of a sliding block can be used for either system.

TUBE LOCK
Used to accommodate small hollow tube made of thin metal and filled with detonating powder. Invented by Joseph Manton of England in 1818 and by Joshua Shaw of Philadelphia, U. S. A., in 1816.

COLT FACTORY—HARTFORD, CONN.

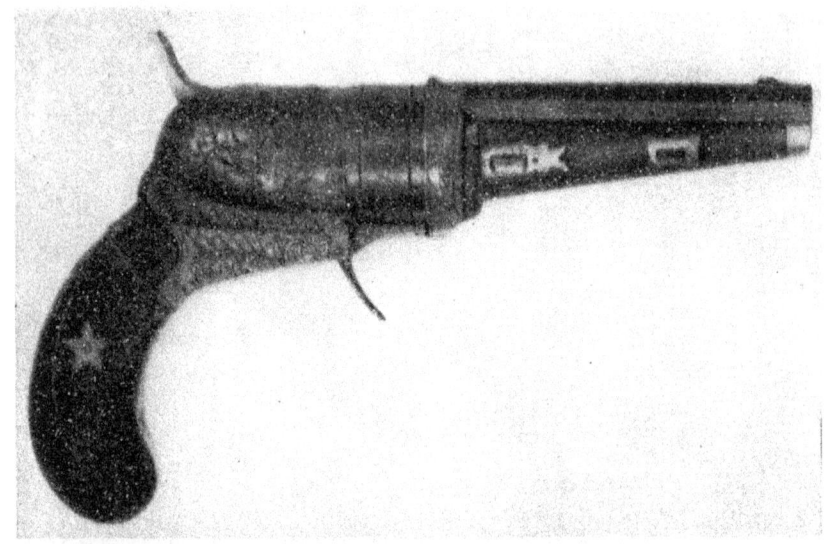

PROMOTION MODEL—1835—CAL. 40; 5 S., 3¼" BBL.
In Wadsworth Athenaeum, Hartford, Conn.

CASED 1839 PATERSON

COLT'S REPEATING PISTOLS,
With the Latest Improvement

No. 1. *Hammer of Pistol.*
2. *Receiver, with five Chambers.*
3. *Trigger.*
D. *Wedge for holding Barrel upon pin.*
4. *Lever or Rammer to ram the ball down with.*

THE PISTOL is first half cocked, or the hammer pulled back to the first notch; then turn the Receiver or Cylinder from left to right, take the powder flask and load the five Chambers, or as many of them as you wish, with Powder; then lay a Ball on the Chamber on the left hand side of the Barrel, turn the Cylinder the same as when you loaded with Powder, so as to get the Ball under the Lever or Rammer, and force the Ball down in the Chamber, and so go on in succession; then put on the percussion caps on the right hand side of the pin head, where a place is cut out for that purpose, and the Pistol is ready for firing, which is done by cocking it and pulling the Trigger; the cocking turns the Cylinder, and brings the Chamber in a line with the Barrel—where, when full cocked, the Cylinder stands firm, but at half cock it revolves.

When you want to clean the PISTOL, which should be done, like every other firearm, as soon as you can after using it—push out the Wedge or Key, and take the Barrel and Cylinder off and wash them well with hot water, clean and dry them well, and put a little oil on the pin on which the Cylinder revolves.

The above is a true representation of the COLT'S PATENT REPEATING PISTOL. Great impositions having lately been practised upon the public by representing and selling the Six Barrel or Self-Cocking Pistol as Colt's Patent Pistol, the public will bear in mind that the Colt's Repeating Pistols, Rifles, Carbines, and Shot Guns, are sold for Cash, at

171 BROADWAY, N-YORK, by
JOHN EHLERS, Proprietor.

1843

COLT'S ADVERTISEMENT—1843

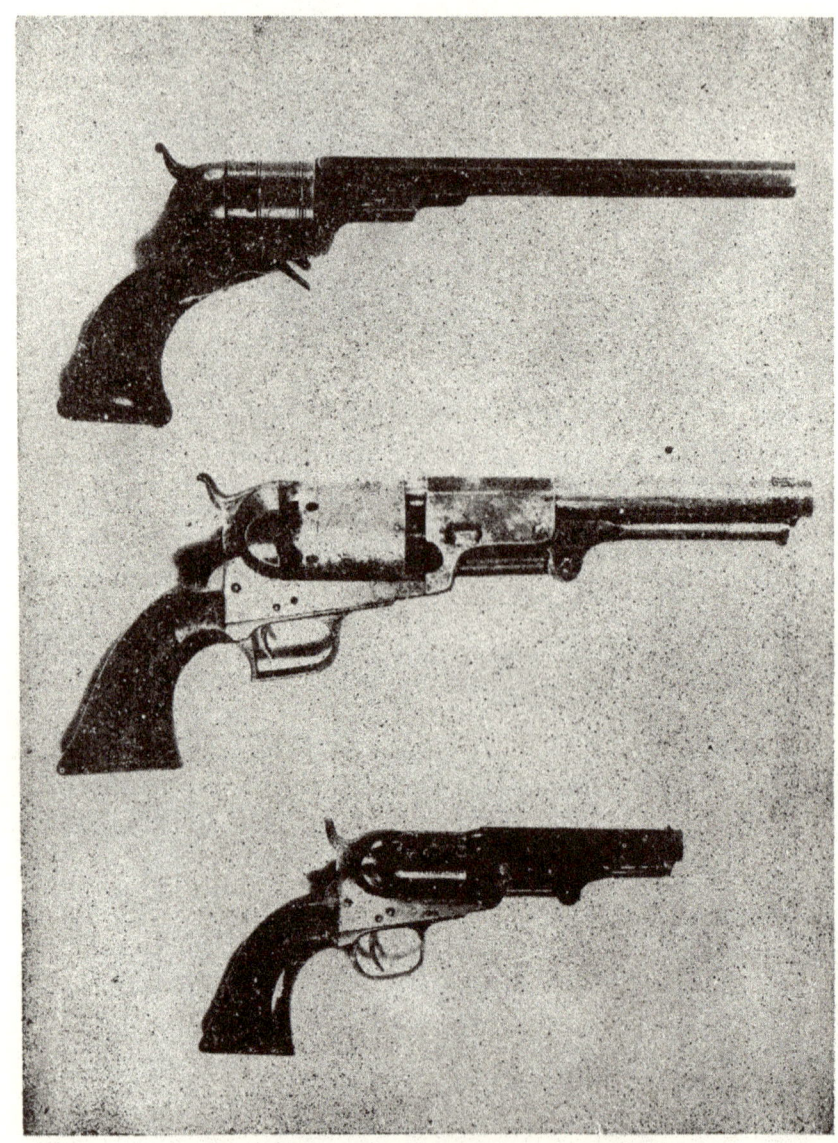
PATERSON-1836 — DRAGOON-1848 — POCKET-1849

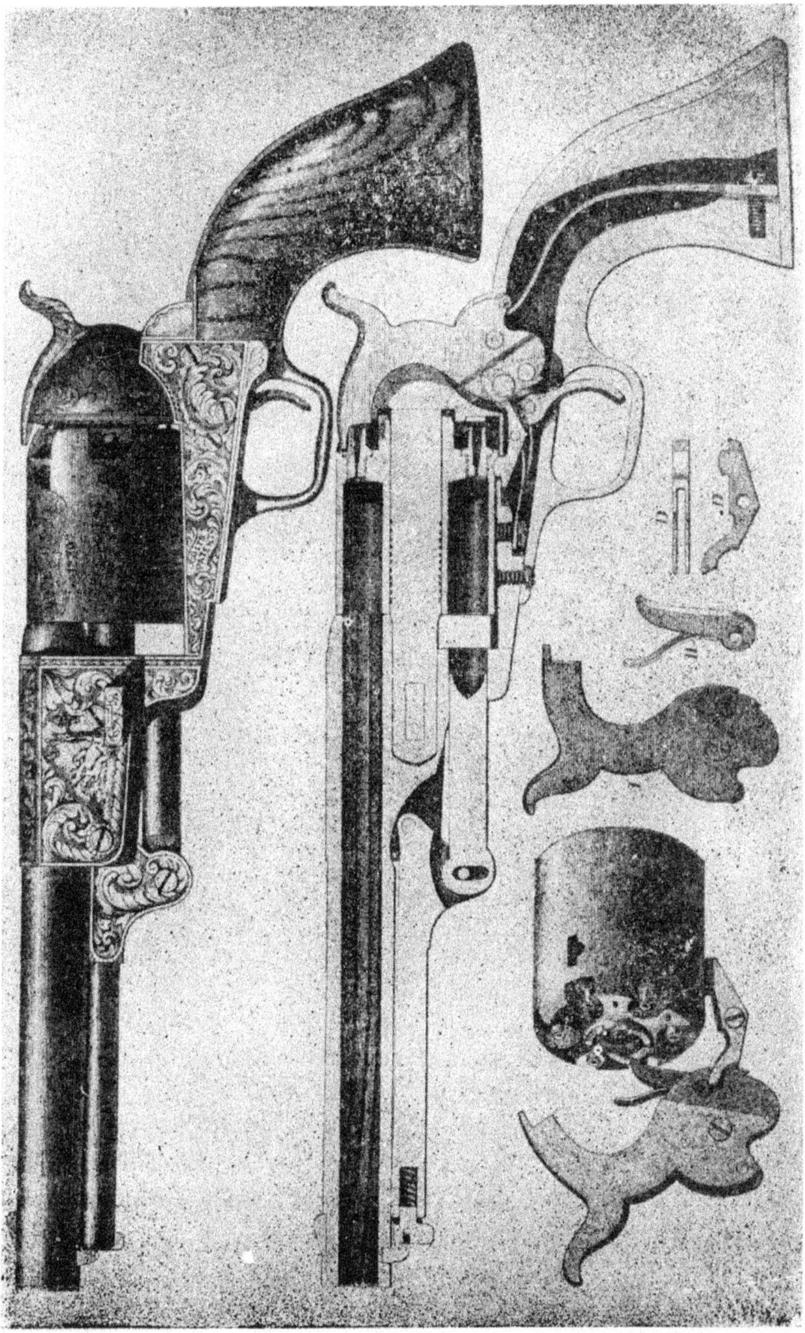

DRAGOON—CROSS SECTION

ADVERTISING CIRCULAR (CIRCA 1850) OF CYLINDER ENGRAVING
1. DRAGOON; 2. NAVY; 3. POCKET MODEL

HANDBOOK OF COLT GUNS

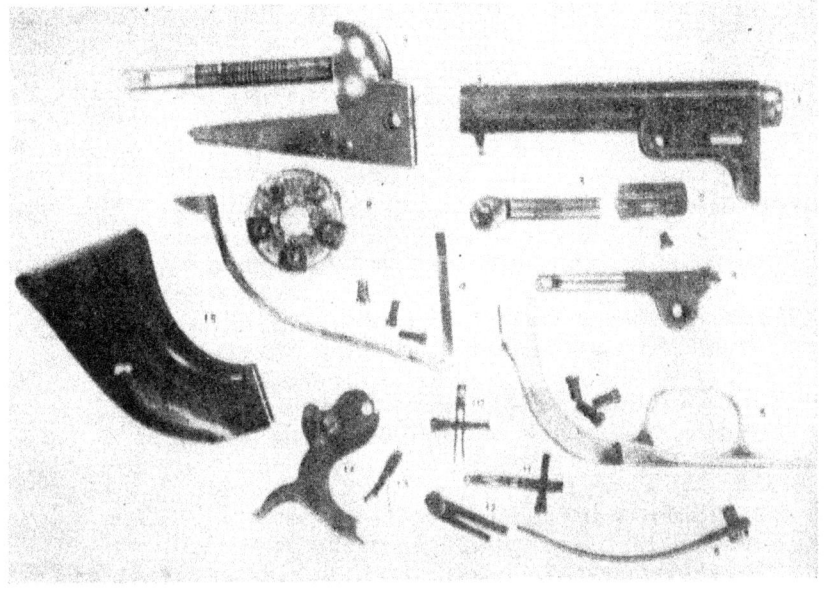

OLD MODEL POCKET PISTOL

1. Barrel
2. Barrel key
3. Ramrod plunger
4. Ramrod lever
5. Trigger guard
6. Mainspring
7. Frame
8. Cylinder
9. Backstrap
10. Cylinder bolt
11. Trigger
12. Trigger spring
13. Hand spring
14. Hammer
15. Grips

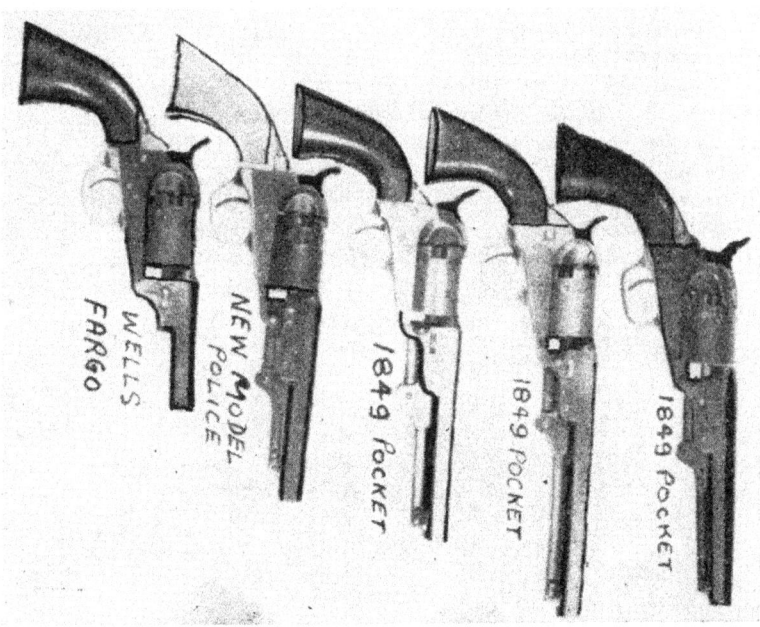

Colt's Patent Fire Arms Manufacturing Co.
HARTFORD, CONNECTICUT.
CARBINES

New Model, Steel Mountings, Rifled Barrels, 18 or 21 inches long;
Six Shots, Caliber or Size of Bore, 36-100ths of an inch diameter
(carrying 42 Elongated or 86 Round Bullets to the pound);
              Weight 8 lbs. 8 oz.,   30.00
Six Shots, Caliber or Size of Bore, 44-100ths of an inch diameter
(carrying 28 Elongated or 48 Round Bullets to the pound);
              Weight 8 lbs. 12 oz.,   32.50
Five Shots, Caliber or Size of Bore, 56-100ths of an inch diameter
(carrying 14 Elongated or 24 Round Bullets to the pound);
              Weight 9 lbs. 8 oz.,   35.00

RIFLES

New Model Steel Mountings, Six Shots, Caliber or Size of Bore, 36-100ths of an inch diameter (carrying 42 Elongated or 86 Round Bullets to the pound):
 Twenty-four inch-Barrel, ... Weight 9 lbs., $32.50
 Twenty-seven inch-Barrel, ... " 10 lbs.,   35.50
 Thirty-inch-Barrel, ... Weight 10 lbs. 8 oz.,   38.50
Same Style, Six Shots, Caliber or Size of Bore, 44-100ths of an inch diameter (carrying 28 Elongated or 48 Round Bullets to the pound):
 Twenty-four inch-Barrel, ... Weight 8 lbs. 15 oz.,   35.00
 Twenty-seven inch-Barrel, . . . " 9 lbs. 2 oz.,   38.00
 Thirty-one and 5-16 inch-Barrel, . . " 9 lbs. 10 oz.,   41.00
Same Style, Five Shots, Caliber or Size of Bore, 56-100ths of an inch diameter (carrying 14 Elongated or 24 Round Bullets to the pound):
 Twenty-four inch-Barrel, ... Weight 8 lbs. 14 oz.,   37.50
 Twenty-seven inch-Barrel, ... " 9 lbs. 11 oz.,   40.50
 Thirty-one and 5-16 inch-Barrel (Pattern used by the U. S. Army),
              Weight 9 lbs. 15 oz.,   43.50

COLT PRICE LIST

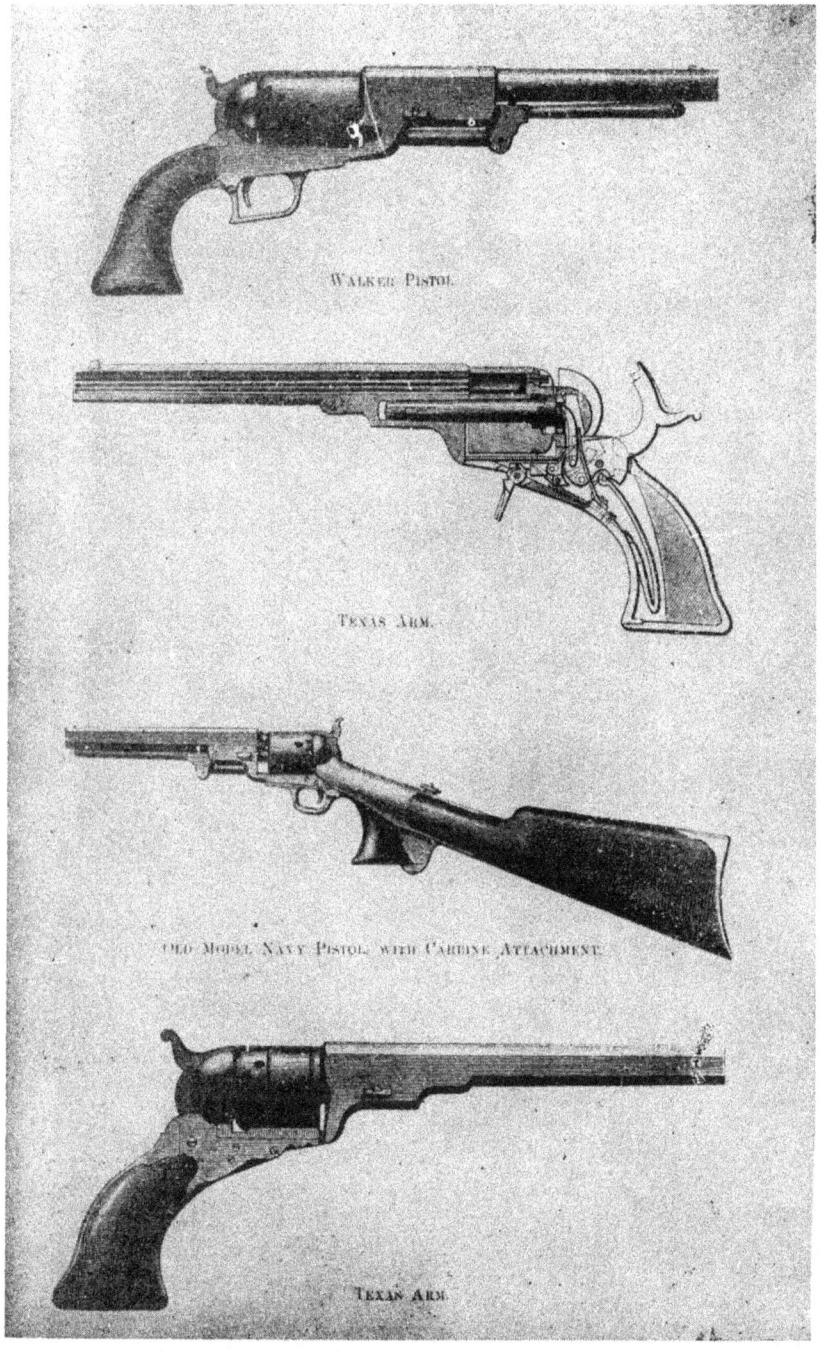

Walker Pistol.

Texas Arm.

Old Model Navy Pistol, with Carbine Attachment.

Texan Arm.

MODEL—1849

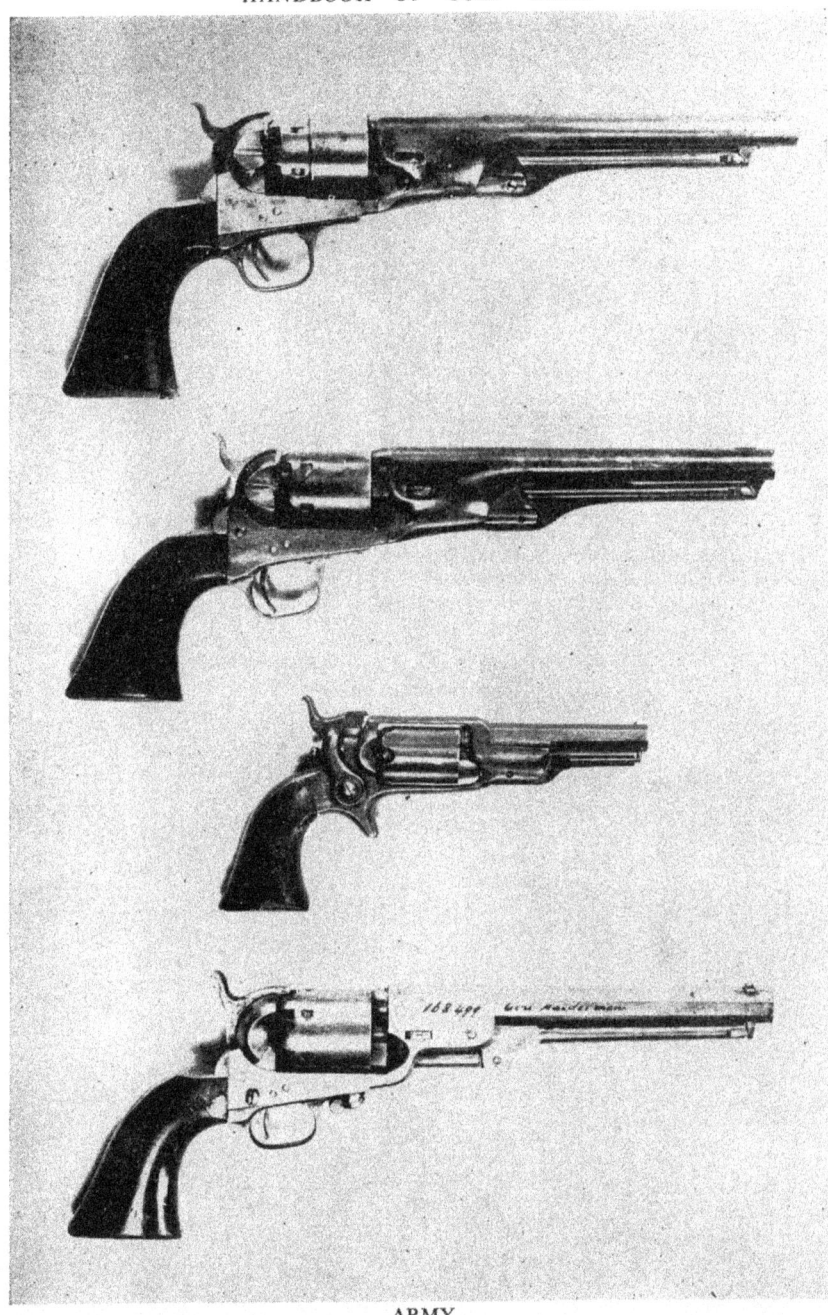

ARMY
NAVY—1861
NEW MODEL POCKET
NAVY—1851

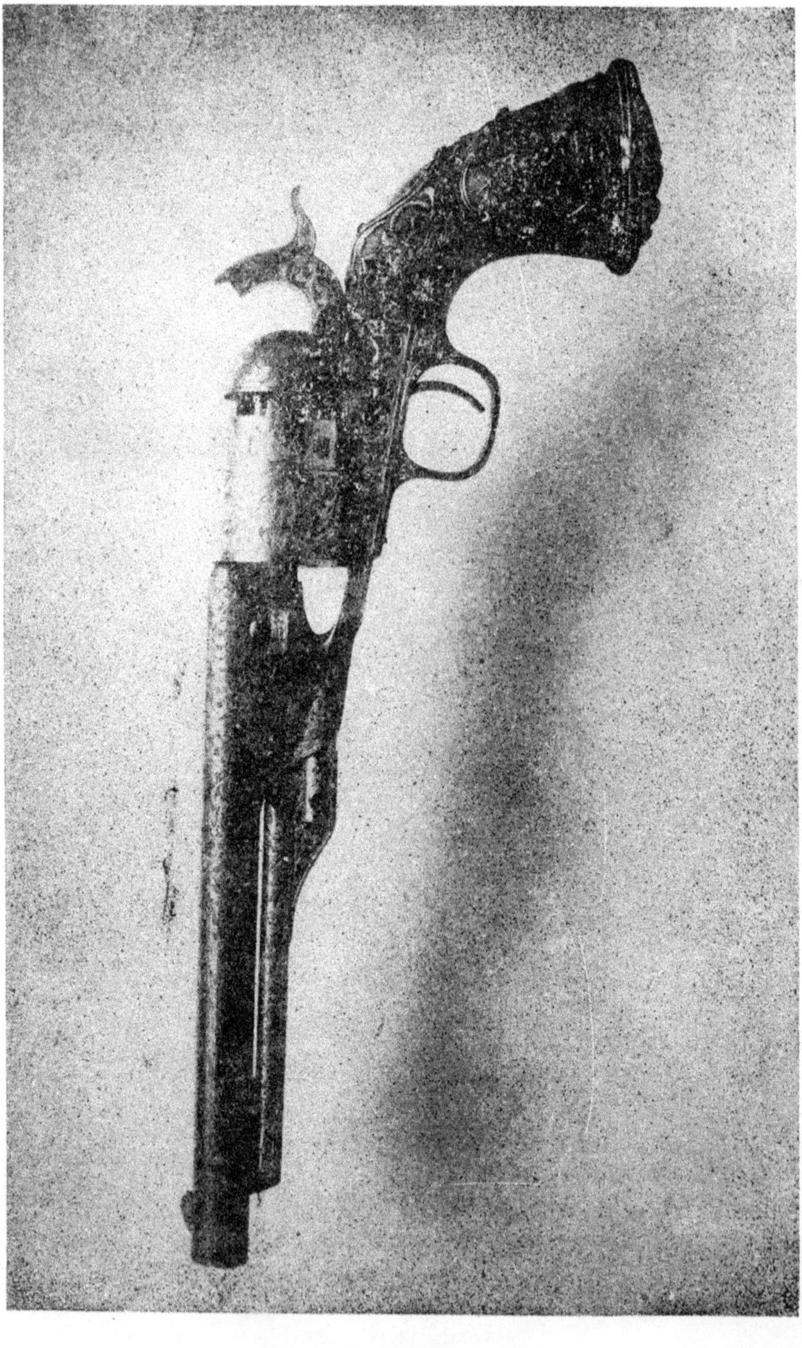

PRESENTATION—MODEL 1860 ARMY

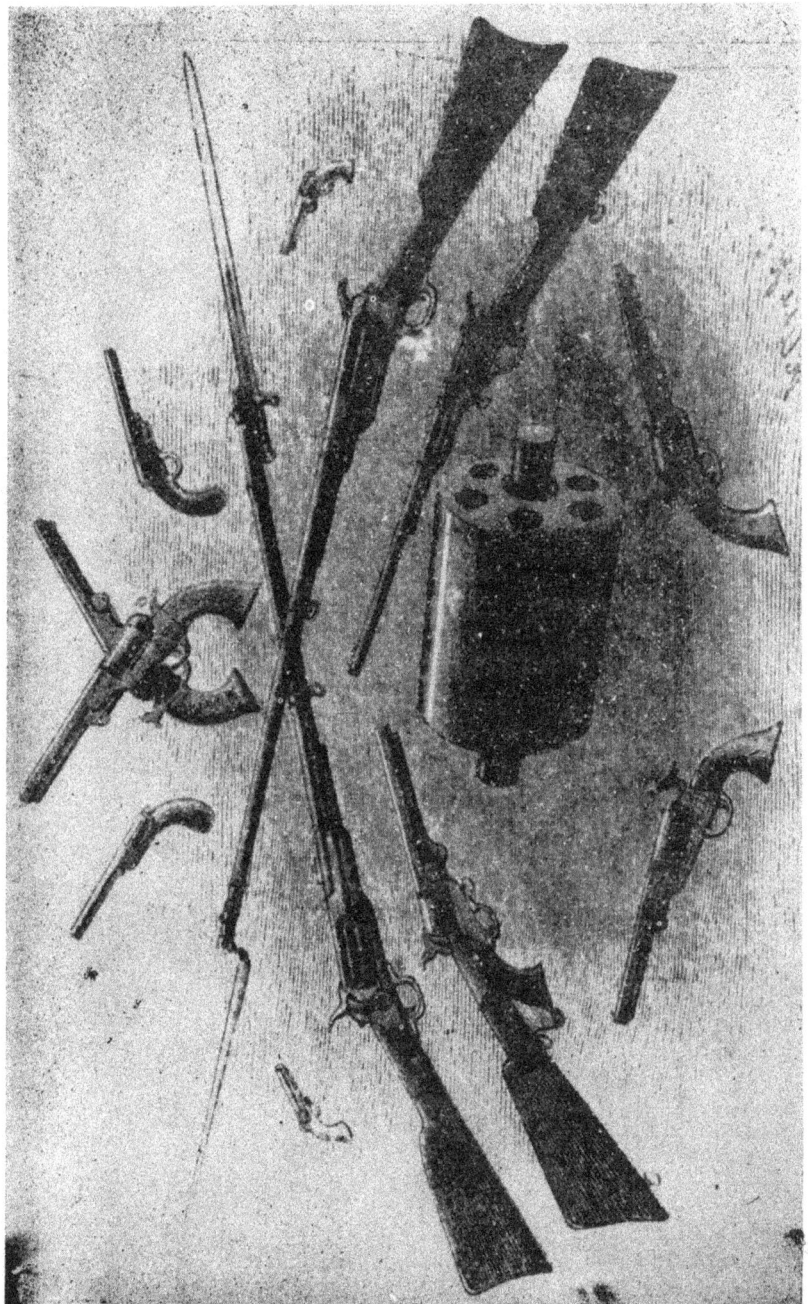

COLT ADVERTISEMENT OF ALL COLT ARMS

Top—Derringer; 41 rf: s.s.; bbl. 2½″ oval flat top; 4½″ long; button right side, 9 oz.; all metal engraved. No. 1.
Center—41 rf; s.s. 2½″ oval flat top bbl.; 5¼″ long; button right side, 9 oz; all metal engraved. No. 2.
Bottom—41 rf; s.s.; bbl. 2½″ round; snap latch; 4½″ long; 7 oz; all metal engraved. No. 3.
Numbers 1 and 2 originally manufactured by National Arms but bought out by Colt arms. Made 1870 to 1890. No. 3 made 1875 to 1912.

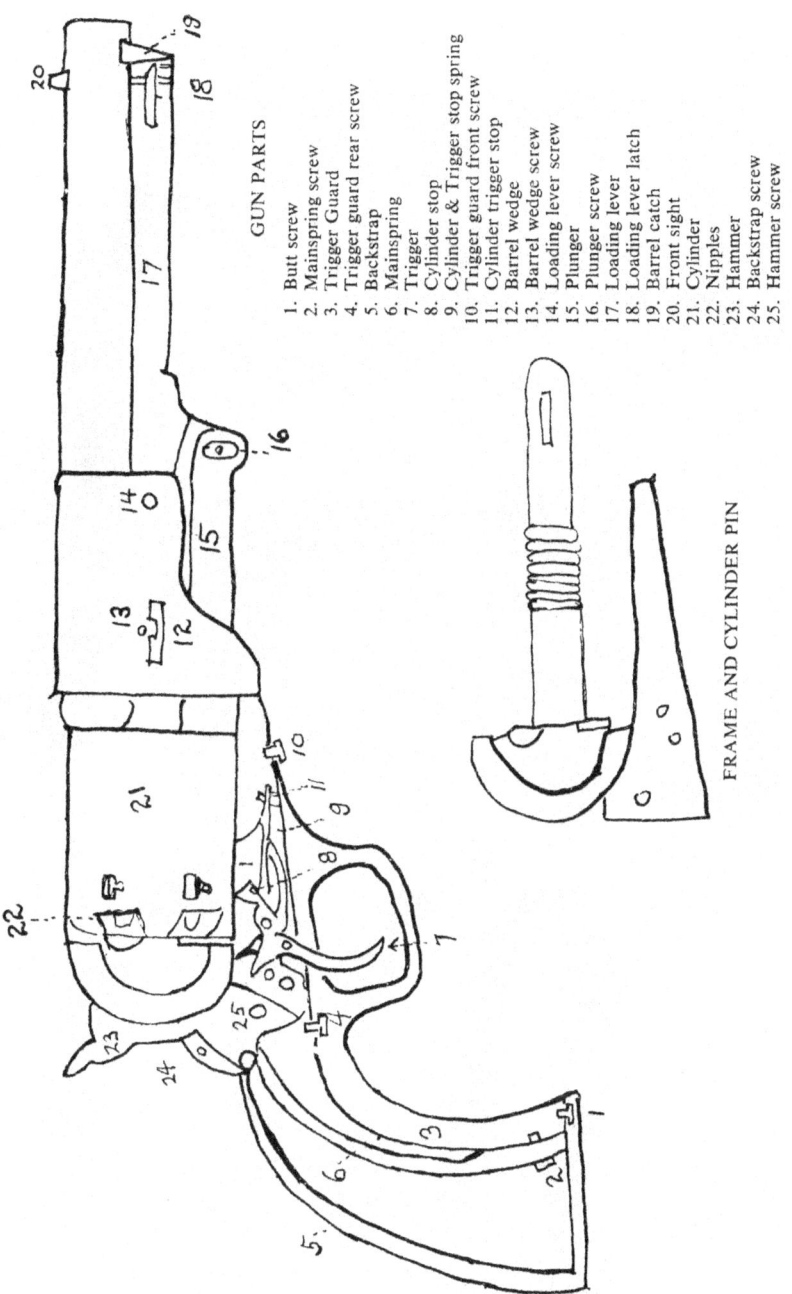

GUN PARTS

1. Butt screw
2. Mainspring screw
3. Trigger Guard
4. Trigger guard rear screw
5. Backstrap
6. Mainspring
7. Trigger
8. Cylinder stop
9. Cylinder & Trigger stop spring
10. Trigger guard front screw
11. Cylinder trigger stop
12. Barrel wedge
13. Barrel wedge screw
14. Loading lever screw
15. Plunger
16. Plunger screw
17. Loading lever
18. Loading lever latch
19. Barrel catch
20. Front sight
21. Cylinder
22. Nipples
23. Hammer
24. Backstrap screw
25. Hammer screw

FRAME AND CYLINDER PIN

1860 ARMY
CONVERSION
1860 ARMY
CONVERSION
1861 NAVY
CONVERSION

ROOT
ROOT
ROOT
ROOT
1855 ROOT

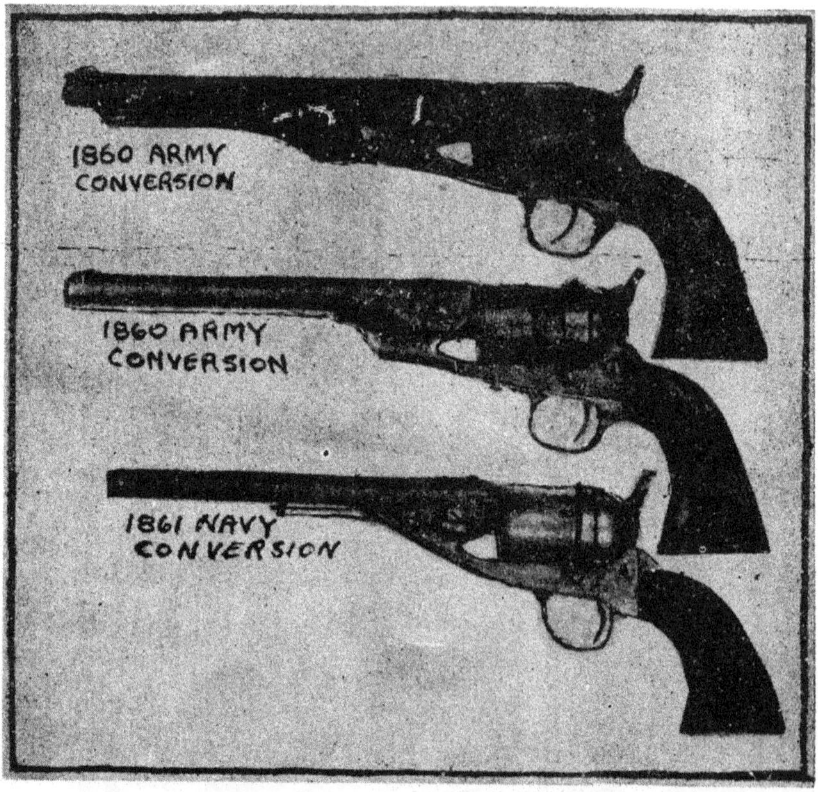

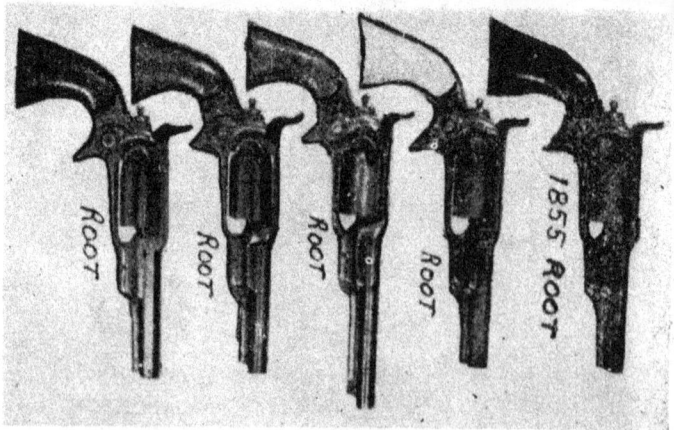

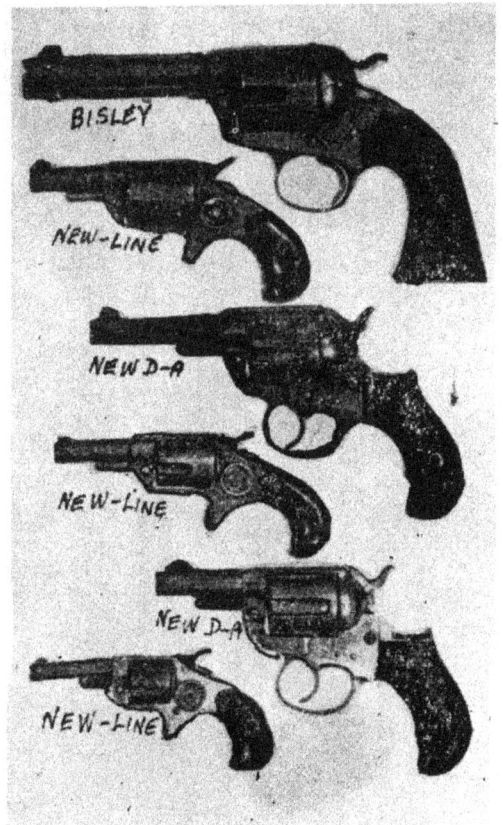

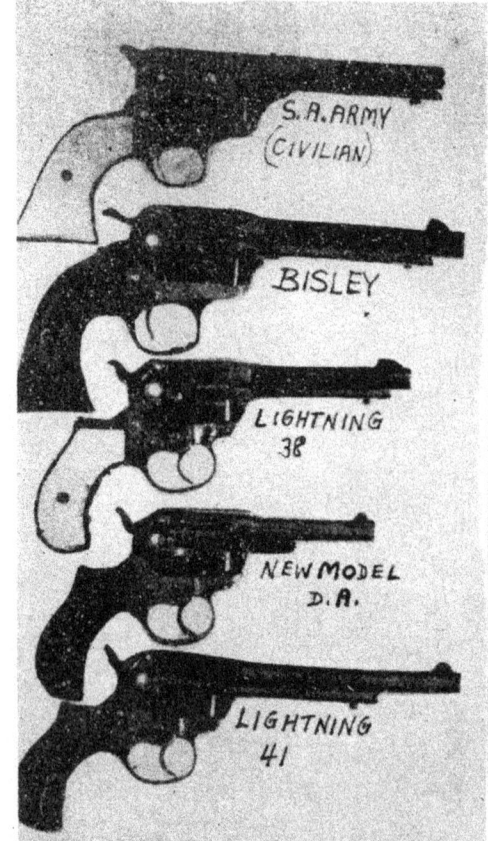

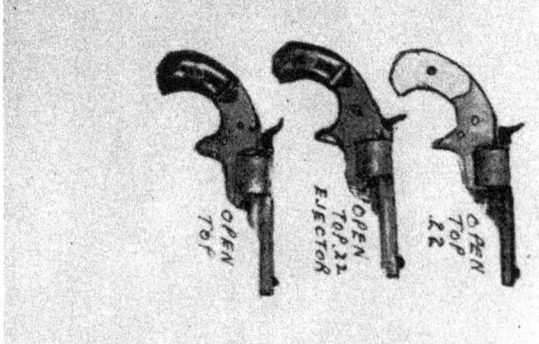

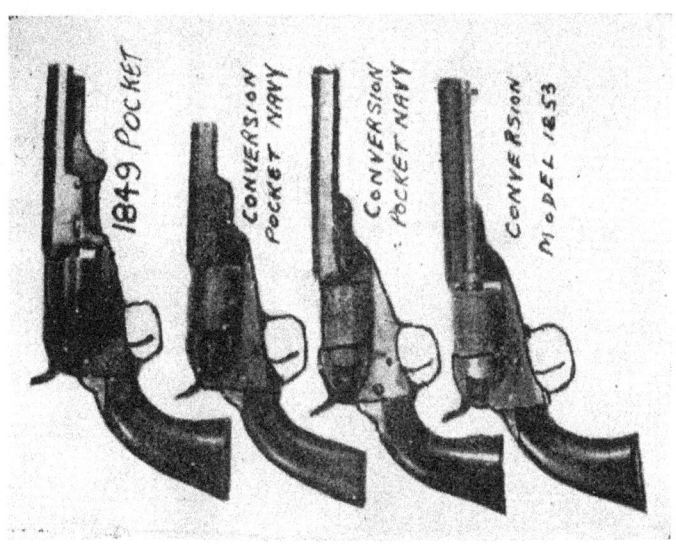

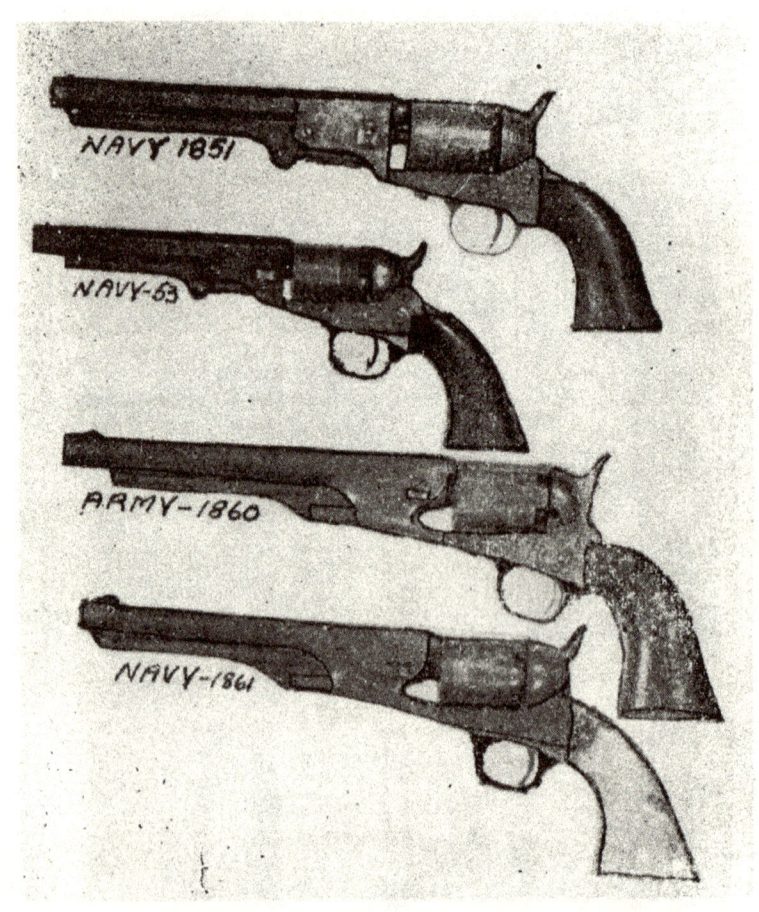

NAVY 1851, NAVY 1853, ARMY 1860, NAVY 1861.

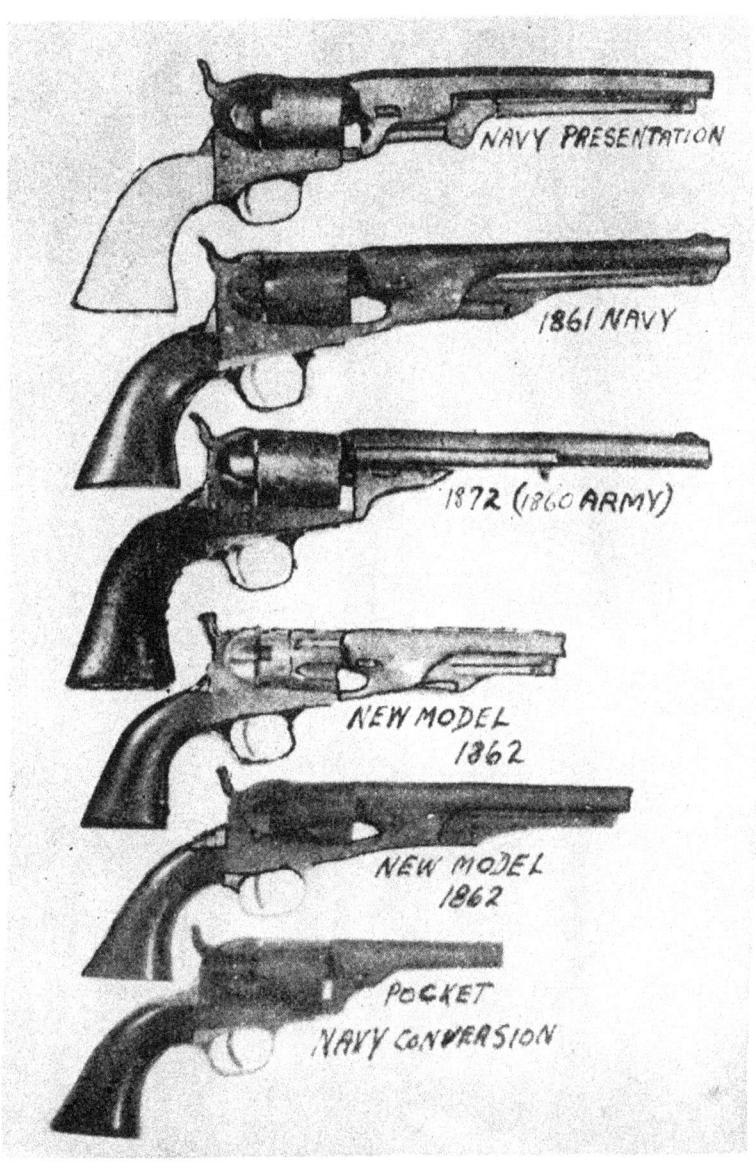

NAVY PRESENTATION, NAVY 1861, ARMY 1872, NEW MODEL 1862, NEW MODEL 1862, POCKET NAVY CONVERSION.

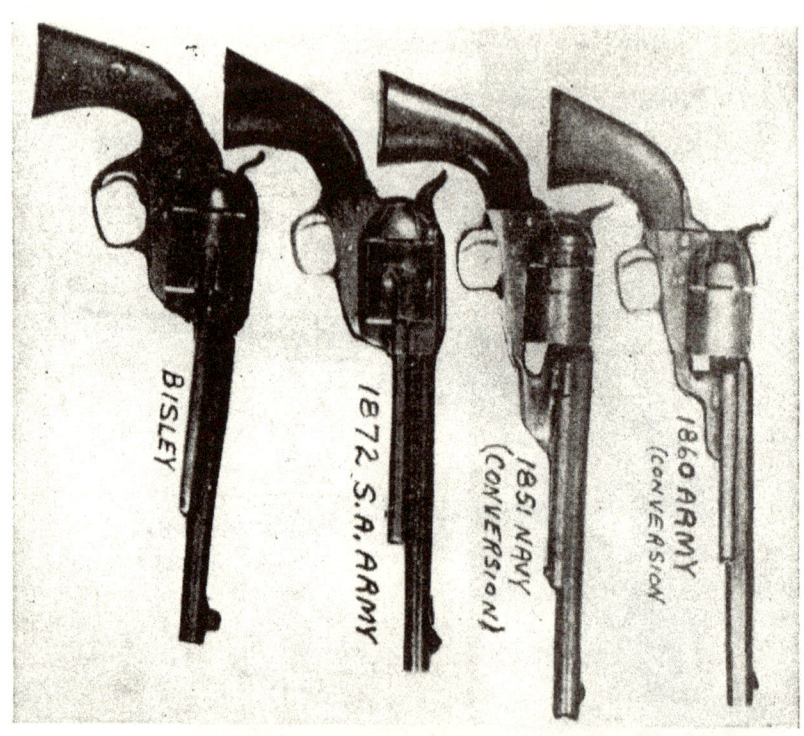

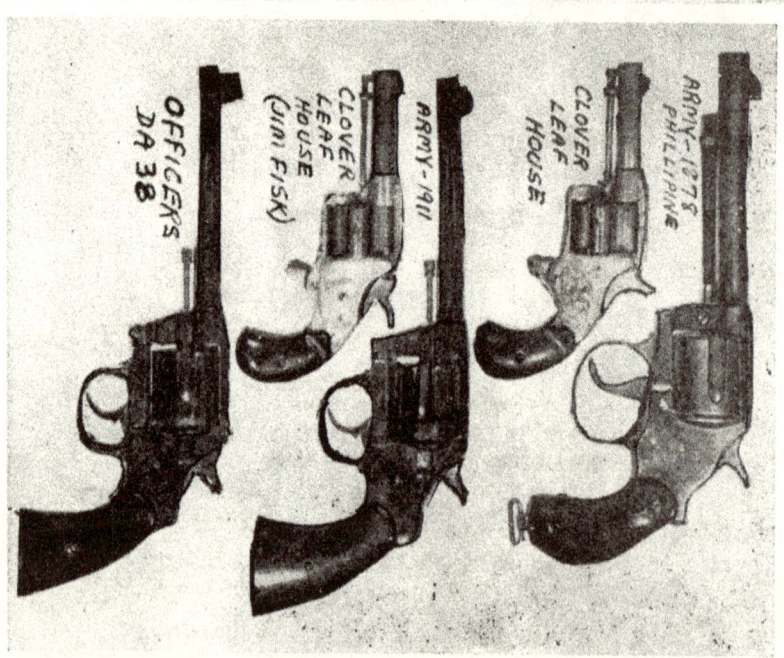

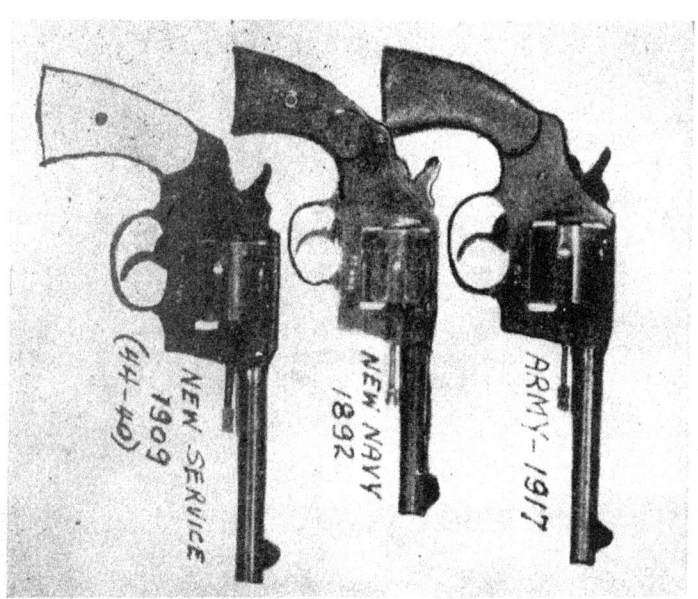

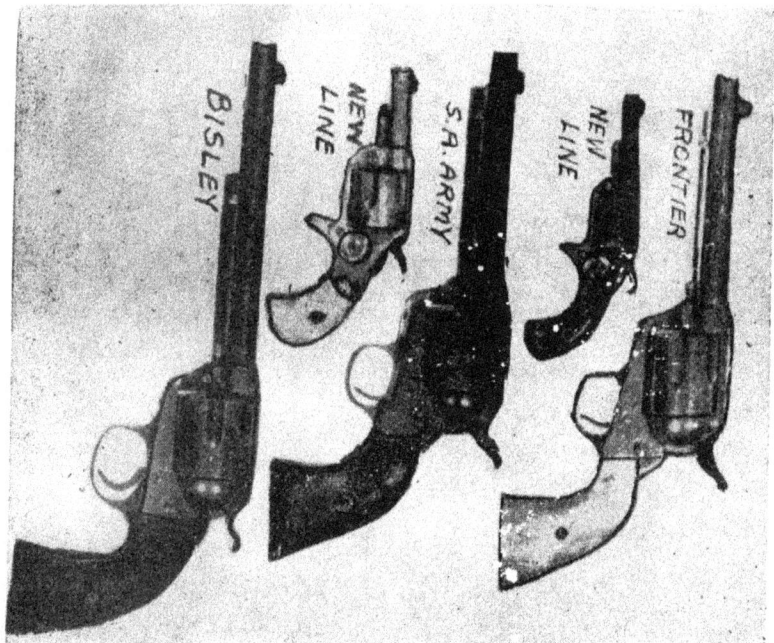

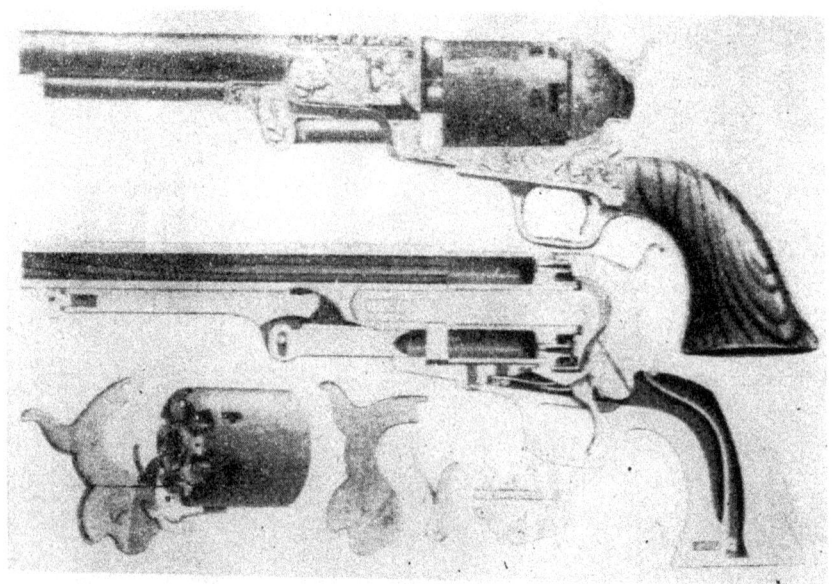

DRAGOON COLT—INTERIOR CROSS-SECTION SIMILAR
TO ANY COLT AFTER 1847 EXCEPT 1855 MODEL

PLATE 18

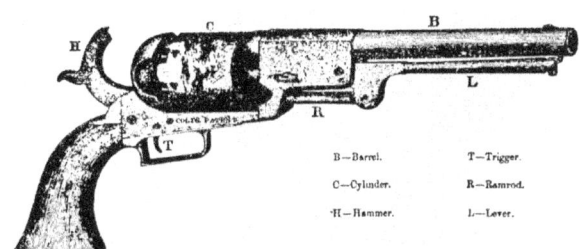

B—Barrel. T—Trigger.
C—Cylinder. R—Ramrod.
H—Hammer. L—Lever.

DIRECTIONS FOR LOADING COLT'S PISTOLS.

First explode a cap on each nipple to clear them from oil or dust, then draw back the hammer to the half-cock, which allows the cylinder to be rotated; a charge of powder is then placed in each chamber, and a ball with the pointed end upwards, without wadding or patch, is put one at a time into the mouths of the chambers, turned under the rammer, and forced down with the lever below the surface of the cylinder, so that they cannot hinder its rotation. This is repeated until all the chambers are loaded. Percussion-caps are then placed on the nipples, when, by drawing back the hammer to the full-cock, the arm is in condition for a discharge by pulling the trigger; a repetition of the same motion produces the like results, viz. six shots without reloading. ☞ The Hammer when at full-cock, forms the sight by which aim is taken.

To carry the arms safely when loaded, the hammer should be let down on one of the pins between each nipple, on the end of the cylinder.

The arm should be thoroughly cleaned and oiled after firing, particularly the base-pin on which the cylinder turns.

Soft lead must be used for the balls. The cylinder is not to be taken off when loaded.

THE QUANTITY OF POWDER USED FOR THE DIFFERENT SIZE PISTOLS.

CAVALRY or HOLSTER PISTOL		1¼,	1½	or	1¾ drachm.
NAVY or BELT	ditto (second size)	½,	⅝	or	¾ ditto
POCKET	ditto (4, 5, and 6 inch barrel)	¼,	⅜	or	½ ditto

Fine-grain Powder the best.

N.B.—It will be safe to use all the Powder the chambers will hold, leaving room for the Ball, whether the Powder is strong or weak.

DIRECTIONS FOR CLEANING.

You must set the lock at half-cock; then drive out the key that holds the barrel and cylinder to the lock-frame—they can be removed; should the barrel stick on the base-pin, the lever may be used to aid in removing it, by forcing the rammer on the partition between the chambers. Take out the nipples. Wash the cylinder and barrel in warm water, dry and oil them thoroughly; oil freely the base-pin on which the cylinder revolves.

TO TAKE THE LOCK TO PIECES, CLEAN, AND OIL.

First—Remove the stock, by turning out the bottom and two rear screws that fasten it to the guard and lock-frame.
Second—Loosen the screw that fastens the mainspring to the trigger-guard, and turn the spring from under the tumbler of the hammer.
Third—Remove the trigger-guard, by turning out the three screws that fasten it to the lock-frame.
Fourth—Turn out the screw, and remove the double spring that bears upon the trigger and bolt.
Fifth—Turn out the screw-pins that hold the trigger and bolt in their places.
Sixth—Turn out the remaining side screw-pin, and remove the hammer with hand attached, by drawing it downwards out of the lock-frame. Clean all the parts and oil them thoroughly.

TO PUT THEM TOGETHER.

Replace the hammer with hand attached, then the bolt, the trigger, the trigger-guard, the mainspring, and finally the handle; returning each of the screws in their proper places, the arm is again fit for use.

Ever faithfully yours, Sam'l Colt

DIRECTIONS FOR USING
COLT'S PISTOLS, RIFLES, CARBINES,
AND SHOT GUNS.

Before loading snap off a round of Percussion Caps to blow the oil and dirt out of the Nipples. Great care should be taken when Colt's Cartridges are not used, that all the Balls are perfect and fit the chambers snugly, otherwise the charges may jar out, and more than one chamber be discharged at once.

For Loading and Firing.

1st. Draw back the Hammer to half-cock, which allows the Cylinder to turn in one direction freely.
2d. Holding the Muzzle erect, place a charge of Powder in, and a Ball upon the mouth of the Chamber.
3d. Turn the Cylinder until the loaded chamber is under the Rammer, and force the Ball with the Lever below the mouth of the chamber. [If the Ball fits, the chamber is then hermetically closed, and the powder protected from water, damp, and sparks of fire.]
4th. Reverse the Arm and place the Percussion Caps upon the Nipples.
5th. Draw the Hammer to full cock, and the Arm is ready for firing.

For Cleaning Old and New Model Army Holster Pistol, 44-100ths Calibre,
Old and New Model Navy or Belt, 36-100ths Calibre, Old Model Pocket, 31-100ths Calibre,
and New Model Pocket, 36-100ths Calibre.

1st. Set the Hammer at half-cock, and drive out the Key or Wedge which holds the Barrel and Cylinder to the Lock-Frame, and remove the parts.
2d. Turn out the bottom and two rear screws which fasten it to the Trigger-Guard and Lock-Frame, and remove the Stock.
3d. Loosen the Screw that fastens the Main-Spring to the Guard, and turn the Spring from under the Hammer.
4th. Turn out the three screws which fasten the Guard to the Lock-Frame, and remove it.
5th. Turn out the Screw, and remove the Double Spring which bears upon the Trigger and Bolt.
6th. Turn out the Side Screws, and remove the Trigger and Bolt.
7th. Turn out the Hammer Screw, and remove the Hammer with the Hand attached, by drawing it downward out of the Lock-Frame. Clean and oil all the parts thoroughly, and restore them to their places in the reverse order of separation.

☞ In ordinary cleaning, set the Hammer at half-cock, and drive out the Key as far as the screw will allow, remove the Barrel, which may be done by the aid of the Lever pressing down the Rammer upon the partitions between the chambers of the Cylinder. Wash the Cylinder and Barrel in warm water, dry and oil them thoroughly, oil freely the Base-pin on which the Cylinder revolves; then replace the parts.

For Cleaning Rifles, Carbines and Shot Guns—all Sizes.

1st. Loosen the Screw in the side of the Frame opposite the Hammer, nearest the head of the Base-pin, set the Hammer at half-cock, press down the Base-pin Catch with the left hand, draw the Base-pin with the right, and remove the Cylinder.
2d. Turn out the Tang and rear Guard-Screws, and remove the Stock.
3d. Turn out the remaining Guard-Screws, and remove the Guard.
4th. Turn out the Screw, detach the Spring from the Stirrup, and remove the Main-Spring.
5th. Turn out the Sear-Spring screw from the under side of the Frame, and remove the Sear-Spring. [For Shot Gun and 56-100ths Calibre Arms, the Sear-Spring is attached to the Guard and need not be removed.]
6th. Turn out the Screw and remove the Trigger.
7th. Turn out the Bolt Screw and remove the Tumbler-Cap.
8th. Turn out the Tumbler Screw, *drive the Tumbler out of the Hammer*, the Bolt and Hand can then be removed.
9th. Turn out the Base-pin Catch Screw and remove the Base-pin Catch.
10th. Drive out the Key and raise the Lever till the Screw is opposite the hole in the Frame, turn out the Screw, remove the Lever and Rammer, and turn out the Barrel. Care should be taken to remove the Lever before turning out the Barrel.

☞ In ordinary cleaning, remove the Cylinder in the manner described above, clean the Cylinder, Barrel, Base-pin and Frame, oil them and replace the parts. To oil the interior of the Lock, remove the Stock and drop in a little oil.

N. B.—To carry the Arms safely, let the Hammer rest upon the Pins or in the Cavities between the Nipples at the rear end of the Cylinder.

COLT'S ARMORY PRINT, HARTFORD, CT.

Coachwhip Publications

CoachwhipBooks.com

Coachwhip
Publications

CoachwhipBooks.com

Coachwhip Publications

CoachwhipBooks.com

Coachwhip Publications

CoachwhipBooks.com

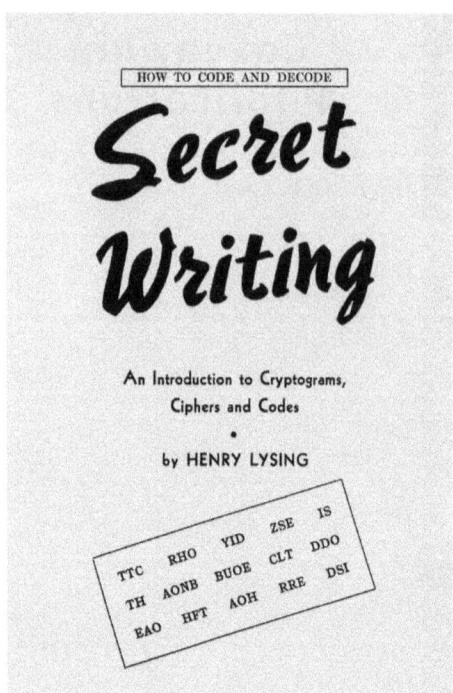

Coachwhip Publications

CoachwhipBooks.com

Coachwhip
Publications

CoachwhipBooks.com

www.ingramcontent.com/pod-product-compliance
Lightning Source LLC
Chambersburg PA
CBHW021009090426
42738CB00007B/717